ENTERTAINING WITH CHILLIES

Mild to Wild: A How To, When To, Why to Chilli Guide for Hosts

Nancy Hillary

DEDICATION

This Chilli Sorceress Book is dedicated to my family.

The secret ingredient to life, and to every perfect meal and event is always Family, Friends, and Love. FFL Forever.

CONTENTS

ENTERTAINING
WITH CHILLIES

INTRODUCTION

Welcome to the Party (Bring Your Tongue and a Towel)

So here we are. You. Me. A book full of chillies. And if your eyebrows are already twitching at the thought of eating something hotter than your ex's temper, you're in the right place.

This isn't some dry culinary lecture written by someone who only ever cooks in lab coats and takes their cumin too seriously. No, this is *Entertaining with Chillies*: a kitchen party in book form, written by a woman who once tried to make hot sauce and ended up with fire in places nobody should have fire.

Let's get one thing straight right off the bat: you don't have to be a trained chef or a spice champion to enjoy this book.

I don't care if your idea of "cooking" is microwaving a ready meal while drinking rosé from a teacup. If you've got taste buds, a sense of humour, and at least one curious friend to share a plate with, you're qualified. What I do care about is showing you how chillies can turn your next meal, dinner party, Tuesday snack binge, or garden BBQ into something people actually remember. Because here's the secret: people don't talk about the perfectly average potato salad. They talk about the dip that made Uncle Gary cry on the porch and then go back for seconds.

This book isn't just about food.

It's about heat with purpose. It's about mixing flavour and flair, about daring your guests to try "just one more bite" while you casually hand them a glass of milk with a smirk.
We'll explore the fun side of fiery—from chilli cocktails to spicy desserts to how to throw a dinner party that's hotter than a summer romance in the Australian Outback.

I'll share recipes that actually work, tips you won't find on those pretentious cooking blogs, and hilarious lessons from my own spicy misadventures. Like the time I mistook a Scotch Bonnet for a harmless bell pepper and spent the evening crying into a bag of frozen peas. You'll also get the lowdown on how different cultures use chillies to connect, celebrate, and show love (or dominance, depending on the dish).

So if you're ready for food that flirts, dips that demand respect, and desserts that bite back, you've found your tribe. Grab your apron, your courage, and possibly a fire extinguisher. It's time to turn the heat on, properly.

ACKNOWLEDGEMENTS

From Braais to Burners, The Chilli Dream That Wouldn't Quit

I still can't quite believe this book is finally sizzling in your hands. What started as a wild idea, somewhere between a fiery boerewors roll and a backstage jalapeño popper, has officially turned into this chilli-drenched reality. And let me be real: I didn't do it alone.

To my incredible circle: you legends nodded and smiled while I raved about hot sauce and spicy business plans. Thank you. You believed it before I fully did. Your faith kept me from jumping ship every time I thought, "Wait... am I really doing this?"

To my superstar cheerleader, Bradleigh, who always beams, "Awesome, Mum!" I love you so much, Punk! Fiona, you jumped in with a dazzling, "How can I help?"—pure gold, thank you. And Brian, who dove in boots and all, ready to make things spicy!

My beautiful family; Stuart, Caroline and Beth, Bradleigh and Caity, Juno, Sable, Lisa, Ben & Fam, John and Nadine, Jasper, Atticus, and Vikki—love you guys.

To my day team: Alice, Amanda, Amy, Divya, Farzana, Jav, Jona, Kelly, Kim, Nargish, Nosheen, Pat U, Pat Z, Theressa—thank you guys for constantly having my back. And to my main team: Wilma, Lora, Maddi, Stuart, Kate, Philippa – thanks for all the extra miles we walk together all the time.

My gorgeous friend Therese, who just assumes I will if I say I will without flinching. Beautiful Belinda, who is always half-packed and ready to fly at the first opportunity.

A huge high-five to all the musos and industry pals who dug deep during the wild Covid days to back my chilli vision, plus Dazzaroo, who's still hounding me for chillies! And, of course, Shanty Spice, my secret weapon—I'm so happy I found you.

I'm an English gal raised on a self-sufficient homestead in South Africa, dreaming of bright city lights. The second I could, I bolted to the live music scene, diving headfirst into the chaos of tour vans and outback servo dinners. If there wasn't a Nando's in sight, no worries—I always had my trusty bottle of chilli sauce, vinegar, or Tabasco tucked in my handbag, ready to flavour-bomb any meal!

Chilli sauce didn't just spice up my food; it lit up backstage chats, boring press conferences, and dull business meetings. Cheesy Jalapeño poppers before a gig at The Shack. Spicy after-gig roadside boerewors rolls. Cold pineapple wedges rolled in chilli spice on the Durban beachfront when we were touring. (Not to forget the epic Bunny Chows.) And of course, every single South African "braai," where no barbecue was complete without a fiery chilli-eating showdown—at least not in my crowd!

Now, in my home in Sydney, Australia, I have a garden full of dozens of chilli varieties, a workshop filled with cooking utensils and magic, and a whole new set of barbecues and backstage areas to light on fire.

When Covid hit and paused my entertainment biz, I seized the moment to dive deep into the vibrant world of chillies. Now, I'm sharing their zesty culture and spicy entertainment vibes with anyone who'll listen—and I'm having an absolute blast! Here's to keeping the chilli love red-hot and making every moment pop with flavour! Come along for the journey; you'll be surprised at just how much you will come to love this fiery little fruit.

Pour a drink, grab a napkin, and let's set your kitchen on fire.

1 SPICE, SPIRIT, AND THE SOCIAL TABLE

You know how some people walk into a room and suddenly everyone straightens their posture, the music sounds better, and even the drinks seem colder? That's what spice does to your food. It's not just an ingredient. It's an entrance. A performance. A bit of culinary theatre. And if your dinner party is a movie, then chilli is the one setting fire to the curtains while the guest's cheer.

This chapter is where we unpack why chillies are the secret MVP of entertaining. We're not here for textbook science or "blah blah Scoville scale" snooze-fests. We're here to talk about why spice brings people together, why it makes a meal memorable, and why your Aunt Carol still talks about that spicy mango salsa you made three Christmases ago that made her hiccup for twenty minutes.

We'll get into the surprising science behind why our brains like the burn, how spice fuels conversation faster than wine, and how to manage your guests' spice tolerance without anyone crying into the hummus. By the end of this chapter, you'll be ready to sprinkle heat like a magician with paprika-stained sleeves.

Why Spice is the Life of the Party

Let me tell you something straight off the grill: bland food has never brought strangers closer. No one bonds over a flavourless couscous. But pass around a bowl of chilli-dusted popcorn and suddenly the room is alive with coughing, laughing, eye-watering chaos, and a unified chorus of, "What is IN this?" That, my friend, is how spice hijacks a gathering, in the best way possible.

Spice isn't just flavour. It's energy. It's the culinary equivalent of a live DJ at a family barbecue. When you serve spicy food, you're not just offering a meal. You're offering an experience. A little shared danger. A communal dare.

When I hosted my first chilli-themed dinner party (which was brave, considering my previous mishap with a Scotch Bonnet and bare hands), I didn't expect the icebreakers to happen over a habanero-laced mango salsa. But there it was. People swapped life stories while guzzling coconut water and playfully blaming each other for who "pushed them" to try the hottest dip. There was giggling, bonding, and the kind of camaraderie you usually only get from assembling IKEA furniture under duress.

Here's the sorcery behind it:

Spice wakes people up. Capsaicin, the active compound in chillies, literally triggers pain receptors. Your body goes, "Uh-oh, danger incoming!" Then it panics, overreacts, and floods you with feel-good endorphins to cope with the perceived threat. It's the same chemical process that makes people enjoy rollercoasters or horror movies (Rozin et al., 2013). It's thrill-seeking… with snacks.

Furthermore, spicy food increases salivation and appetite, which naturally makes people hungrier and more engaged (McGee, 2004). In short? Chilli makes food taste more alive and moreish. It's not just "tasty." It's chase-you-around-the-plate addictive.

From a hosting perspective, spicy food also encourages pacing. Think about it. Nobody wolfs down a mouthful of fire and leaps for the next bite like it's lukewarm rice pudding. They sip, pause, discuss. You create moments of anticipation and relief, which means your dinner stretches longer and flows more naturally. And that's what great hosts want, right? Not just full bellies, but stories.

There's even research showing that people who enjoy spicy food tend to be more adventurous and sociable (Byrnes & Hayes, 2013). That's right. Chilli people are the life of the party. They laugh louder, talk longer, and lean into their food (and their lives) with a little more zing.

So, when you add spice to your menu, you're doing more than showing off your culinary flair. You're setting the tone. You're saying, "This won't be a beige night." You're inviting your guests to join you in something a bit bold, a bit cheeky, and a little unpredictable.

The Science Behind the Sizzle

So, we've established that spice doesn't just wake up your taste buds; it wakes up the whole room. But what exactly is going on inside your body when you eat something that feels like it could qualify as arson? Why does your tongue tingle, your nose run, and your eyes water like you've just watched the end of *The Notebook*, while at the same time, you're grinning and reaching for more?

Let's break it down.

The hero (or villain, depending on your tolerance) in this story is a little chemical troublemaker called capsaicin. It's the compound found in chillies that tricks your body into thinking it's on fire. But here's the twist: there's no actual burn.
No flames.
No damage.
Just pure, delicious deception.

Capsaicin binds to your TRPV1 receptors, these little gatekeepers in your mouth and digestive tract whose job is to detect heat (Caterina et al., 1997). When capsaicin shows up, those receptors throw their arms in the air and scream, "INCOMING!" So your body reacts accordingly: flushed skin, quickened heartbeat, watering eyes, and the sudden need to fan yourself with whatever napkin, coaster, or neighbour's menu is available.

But the plot thickens. Once your body gets over the panic, it releases a cocktail of endorphins—natural painkillers that come with a side of pleasure. That "high" people talk about after eating spicy food? It's real. It's biochemical. And it explains why people voluntarily sign up to chew on Carolina Reapers like they're chasing glory on a game show. Pain turns into pleasure. Torture becomes triumph.

Now, here's where things get even more fun.
That flush you feel? The sweating? The increased heart rate? It's called gustatory sweating, and it's part of why spicy food feels like a workout without the gym membership. Some researchers even believe spicy food can temporarily boost metabolism and curb cravings (Ludy et al., 2012). So yes, technically, your third helping of peri-peri chicken might be helping your waistline. You're welcome.

Let's not ignore digestion, either. Spicy food can stimulate gastric juices, helping digestion in small doses. But go too far and, well, your bathroom might hold a grudge. That's why balance is key. I once went on tour in Northern South Africa and made the rookie error of downing a dish labelled "for locals only." By the time dessert came, I was crying into a mango and begging my intestines for forgiveness.

Here's the good news:

Your tolerance can improve. Just like building muscle, your spice endurance can grow with regular (and joyful) exposure. That means your guests who shy away from anything above black pepper today may be joyfully dunking wings into ghost pepper sauce a few months from now. Small steps. Big flavour.

Chillies as Conversation Starters

We just unpacked how capsaicin plays trickster with your taste buds and flirts with your nervous system like a salsa dancer with something to prove. But spice isn't just an internal fire; it's social fuel. A plate of chilli-laced nachos can do what a whole shelf of small talk books never could: break the ice faster than a Labrador at a beach party.

You see, spicy food doesn't let people sit in awkward silence. It demands a reaction. One bite of a jalapeño-stuffed empanada and suddenly your quiet cousin is recounting that time she accidentally drank chilli vodka thinking it was water.

I once watched two strangers bond over a shared plate of kimchi dumplings, eyes watering, laughing, comparing survival strategies. No polite weather chat. No awkward pauses. Just the universal language of, "Oh wow... did you just eat that whole thing?"

Here's the magic behind it:

Eating spice is a shared risk. It's culinary roulette. And when people take risks together, even tiny ones like daring to try the "spicy sauce only locals touch," they bond. It's science. A study in *Appetite* found that spicy food increases emotional arousal and social bonding, especially when eaten in group settings (Zandstra et al., 2016). Translation? Sweat builds solidarity.

Not to mention, spicy food creates a sort of one-upmanship that's weirdly wholesome.

You don't need to be rich, stylish, or charming to win a chilli challenge. You just need stubborn taste buds and the will to suffer publicly. I've watched quiet accountants transform into local legends because they downed a ghost pepper wing without flinching. There's pride in pain, and people love a comeback story—especially when someone cries, survives, and then goes back for seconds.

And then there are the stories. Oh, the stories. Spicy food is a conversation starter that keeps giving long after the last bite. People love recounting how their mouth betrayed them: how they tried to act cool, failed miserably, and earned the respect of the table anyway. And you, the clever host, were the ringmaster of that spicy circus. You orchestrated an experience, not just a meal.

Want a guaranteed way to jump-start a dull gathering? Set out a "Chilli Flight": a mild-to-wild lineup of sauces or snacks. Guests will hover around it like moths to a flamethrower. They'll sniff, sample, hesitate, dare, and cheer each other on. It's communal drama in edible form. No icebreakers required, and way more fun than beer pong!

Spice Levels: Setting the Mood, Not Setting Off Alarms

Now that we've talked about how chillies break the ice better than a badly timed political joke at a family reunion, let's switch gears. Because while laughter, bonding, and a shared love for masochistic munching is great, nobody wants a dinner party that turns into a survival challenge. I'm not trying to brag, but I once served a mango-habanero dip so fiery that my neighbour texted me the next morning asking if taste buds grow back. So, trust me when I say: spice needs boundaries.

Here's the golden truth.

Not everyone wants to sweat through their shirt while eating finger food. Some guests want a gentle nudge, not a punch to the palate. So as the host, you get to be the spice conductor. You're not just serving food. You're setting the rhythm. You're building trust. And you're definitely trying to keep Grandma from mistaking Scotch Bonnet sauce for apricot jam.

Spice isn't about going full nuclear. It's about build and balance. Think of it like flirting. You don't open with a marriage proposal. You build tension. You tease. You coax. You leave them wanting more without needing paramedics. A well-designed spicy menu takes guests on a journey, from a little tickle to a cheeky slap to a satisfying zing—never straight to the dragon's breath of doom.

The trick?

Offer options. Start with mild crowd-pleasers: sweet chilli jam, smoky chipotle dips, crispy jalapeño poppers that whisper, not scream. Then, slowly and subtly, introduce bolder flavours. Maybe a harissa hummus or peri-peri skewers. Keep the truly dangerous stuff (I'm looking at you, Carolina Reaper hot sauce) labelled, isolated, and treated with the same caution you'd give a live grenade wrapped in clingfilm.

I once hosted a "Heat Ladder" dinner where each course got progressively spicier. We had cooling mocktails and yoghurt-based dips alongside every dish, just in case someone hit their limit. By dessert, we'd only lost two guests to the backyard hammock, and one of them came back stronger. The others? Legends with taste buds forged in fire.

Also, a pro tip from my sorceress's book of spells: make sure your guests know what they're biting into. Label sauces. Mention heat levels. Use colour coding, tiny flags, or a chalkboard heat chart that ranges from "sassy" to

"Satan's armpit." People appreciate clarity when the difference between mild and mouth-melting can be a single bite.

SMOKED
PAPFIKKA
GINGER
GRIN

2 THE CHILLI SORCERESS'S PANTRY

Now that you've survived the social singe of Chapter 1, it's time to peek behind the curtain. Welcome to my pantry. The sacred chamber. The nerve centre of my spice-fuelled mischief. This is where the real magic happens.

Because here's the truth: great spicy food doesn't start at the table. It starts on the shelf. If you think flavour just happens in the pan, that's like believing Beyoncé rolls out of bed in full costume with backup dancers. It's prepped, layered, planned. And it begins right here, with a shelf full of misbehaving jars and bottles that could start a coup in the right pot of stew.

You don't need a gourmet spice rack that looks like an Instagram ad for kitchen envy. But you do need some essentials. A few firecrackers. Some undercover heroes. Maybe one or two jars that smell like vengeance and taste like glory.

In this chapter, I'm taking you into my world. From bell peppers to Carolina Reapers. From innocent pastes to bottled war crimes. You'll learn which chillies do what, how to stock your shelves like a culinary trickster, and how to use spice with intention.

Chillies 101 – From Bell to Reaper

If you've ever stared at a wall of chillies in the supermarket and thought, "Why does one look like a wrinkled raisin, one looks like it's about to sue me, and the other smells like nothing but chaos?", you're not alone. Chillies are a wild bunch. They're the punk rockers of the produce aisle: unpredictable, flashy, and sometimes dangerous. But once you know who's who, the game changes completely.

Before we get into spice-laced sauces and cheeky chutneys, we need to meet the gang.

Starting with the big softie: the bell pepper. No heat, all heart. Perfect for those who want the glamour of a chilli without the commitment. Great in colour, crunchy in character, and ideal when you want to flirt with fire but not get burned.

Now, move a little up the naughty scale and you meet the jalapeño. The people pleaser. Reliable, respectful, and still capable of a bit of a bite when roasted or pickled. Then you get its sassier cousins: serranos, cayennes, and Thai bird's eyes. These are the chillies that don't ask permission. They announce themselves.

And then, like any decent soap opera, you've got the villains. The ones you don't invite to your grandma's potluck: ghost peppers, Scotch bonnets, the infamous Carolina Reaper.

But it's not just about heat.

Each chilli has its own voice. Some are smoky, like the deep-throated jazz singers of the spice world. Others are sharp, citrusy, fruity, and earthy. A habanero, for instance, has a surprising tropical sweetness under that high-octane heat—like a dangerous fruit cocktail wearing stilettos.

What helps is understanding the Scoville scale, the official measuring stick of chilli heat. Bell peppers sit at a docile zero. Jalapeños range between 2,500 to 8,000 units. Ghost peppers? Somewhere in the "why would you do that to yourself?" region of 1 million. Carolina Reapers? Clocking in at over 2.2 million. That's not seasoning. That's a dare.

Now, before you panic and start Googling "chilli antidotes," remember this: you are not required to use the hotshots. Most delicious, practical entertaining spells land comfortably between bell and habanero. The drama is optional. The flavour is forever.

And while some chillies dry better than your ex's sense of humour, others shine fresh or pickled. Knowing which to use where is like knowing when to wear heels and when to bring flats. Important. Impactful. And very much worth learning.

Spicy Staples Every Host Needs

So, now that you've met the chilli family, from the bell-bottomed peacekeeper to the Reaper that whispers threats into your soup, it's time we talk about your armoury. The staples. The non-negotiables. The chilli-sidekicks that should be in every halfway decent kitchen if you plan on throwing a party with a pulse.

This isn't about hoarding a dozen random sauces with labels in seven languages and a best-before date that predates your last holiday romance. No. We're building a lineup. Reliable. Bold. Spicy, but with manners.

Let's start with the obvious: hot sauce. Every host needs a good one. Not the watery stuff that tastes like vinegar with an anger problem. I'm talking about a balanced sauce with heat, tang, and a personality.

Sriracha is a classic if you're new to the game. It's the Beyoncé of hot sauces: popular, smooth, and works with everything from eggs to noodles. But branch out. Try a smoky chipotle one or a tangy Caribbean-style scotch bonnet bottle. They hit differently. They flirt before they bite.

Then there's chilli flakes. They look innocent, but sprinkle too generously and your guests will be coughing their regrets into their cocktails.

A friend of mine, let's call her Julia, once threw a dinner party and mistook her "mild Italian herb mix" jar for crushed red chillies. Long story short, her guests were silently weeping over lasagne and chugging Pinot Grigio like it was Holy Water. By dessert, they'd formed a support group and a group chat named "Flames of 2019."

Next: chilli oil. Oh, the glory. A drizzle of this over roasted veg, noodles, pizza, even vanilla ice cream (yes, you read that right), and you've got yourself a crowd pleaser. It adds heat with glamour. Think of it as the lipstick of your spice cabinet. A tiny touch makes everything look, and taste, more alive.

Let's not forget smoked paprika. Technically not spicy, but she brings depth like a jazz singer in a smoky lounge. A sprinkle on devilled eggs or a rub for grilled meats turns "meh" into "wow, who are you and why haven't you been cooking for me all along?"

And if you're feeling bold, invest in a fermented chilli paste like gochujang or sambal oelek. These are not your everyday condiments. These are flavour bombs. Add a teaspoon to a marinade or stir-fry and suddenly your Tuesday leftovers are giving Michelin-star energy.

Don't feel pressured to collect them all like Pokémon. Start with two or three. Let your taste guide you. Host a tasting night. Mix and match. Let your guests vote for their favourite "sauce of the night." It's fun, interactive, and gives your less confident cooks a chance to engage without the pressure of a spatula in hand.

The Power of Pastes, Powders & Preserves

If spicy staples are the life of the pantry party, then pastes, powders, and preserves are the secret agents in sequinned cloaks. They don't just show up; they transform dishes. Quietly, decisively, and without begging for attention. These little powerhouses take your cooking from "fine" to "was this catered?"

We've already flirted with chilli oils and saucy affairs. But pastes and powders? These are your flavour architects. They're what make the difference between a flat dish and a layered masterpiece. It's like the difference between a handshake and a well-timed wink.

Let's start with pastes.

These are often fermented, concentrated, and unapologetically bossy. They arrive in a tiny jar but carry the energy of a five-person mariachi band. Take gochujang, for instance. It's a Korean chilli paste made from red pepper powder, fermented soybeans, and sticky rice. It's sweet, spicy, salty, and slightly funky, in the best way. A spoonful in a stew or marinade? Game changer. Or harissa, the North African queen of pastes: smoky, deep, slightly floral. You can stir it into couscous or smear it on a roast chicken and instantly look like you know exactly what you're doing (even if you just Googled "how to roast chicken" ten minutes earlier).

Powders, on the other hand, are your speed dial to intensity. You've got cayenne, chilli powder blends, ancho, aleppo, chipotle—each with their own mood and message. Chipotle says, "I've been smoked near a bonfire while reading poetry." Cayenne says, "Buckle up." And ancho whispers, "Deep earthy notes coming through, don't rush me."

Then we have preserves. These are the long-game players. Pickled chillies, fermented sauces, even chilli jams. If you've never tasted a mature cheddar toastie with a dollop of homemade chilli jam, I need you to stop reading and fix that situation immediately. Preserves add brightness and heat without steamrolling your dish. They show up late but always make an entrance.

Now, these ingredients play incredibly well with others. Mix a bit of harissa paste with Greek yoghurt and you've got a dip that'll make people write poems in your honour. Add chipotle powder to melted butter and drizzle over popcorn. Suddenly your movie night has teeth.

One of my friends, Marcus, once accidentally discovered a chilli marmalade in a gift basket. He was too lazy to find a cracker, so he slapped it on roast pork. To this day, it's the only dish his in-laws specifically request. Sometimes magic happens when you stop trying to be clever and just open the damn jar.

A word of caution from my sorceress's grimoire: not all pastes and powders are created equal. Some are saltier. Some are louder. Some should only be invited to small gatherings. Taste-test first. And always, always store them properly. Your chilli powder should not smell like despair and cardboard. If it does, bin it.

Balancing Heat with Flavour (and Not Regret)

We've played with powders. We've romanced pastes. We've preserved like pantry pirates on a spice crusade. Now comes the part where we face the most misunderstood creature in chilli sorcery: balance.

Because flavour without control is just culinary chaos. It's standing in stilettos on a cobbled street during a rainstorm while juggling flaming pineapples. Impressive, yes, but wildly unsafe.

You see, the chilli world has a devil. And its name is Ego.

Ego is the demon that whispers, "More heat means more skill." Ego is what convinced Tom (real human, not a metaphor) to drop a whole dried ghost pepper into his famous stew without so much as a taste test. Tom, bless him, wanted to impress his new girlfriend, who said she liked "spicy food." What she meant was "Nando's medium." What Tom served her was a bowl of volcanic punishment. She cried. He cried. The neighbours heard things. The relationship lasted exactly three more dates, none of which involved food.

Let me say it straight: spicy food is not a competition unless you're in a pub car park with a microphone and a waiver form. It's not about overpowering. It's about partnership. Heat should lift a dish, not burn the house down while stealing your insurance papers.

Let me introduce you to the Demon of Overcompensation. It wears an apron, winks at your guests, and says, "Wait till you try my Reaper rub." It believes more chilli equals more bravery. But in reality? It kills complexity. It buries subtleties. It's the reason half the population thinks spicy food is just pain dressed up in cumin.

You don't need to go nuclear to earn respect. In fact, the real flex is control. A dish that builds heat, that lingers, teases, dances just close enough to the edge without diving headfirst into disaster—that's where the power lives.

Balancing heat means knowing your ingredients. It means tasting as you go. It means remembering that fat, acid, sugar, and salt are your allies. They calm the storm, round the edges, and smooth the spike. Ever added a splash of lime to a spicy salsa? Or a dollop of cream to a vindaloo? That's balance. That's grace.

Even pro chefs learn to respect this. David Chang (yes, *that* David Chang) once admitted he had to unlearn the idea that chilli was just about impact. He learned to use it like a scalpel, not a sledgehammer.

So here's your permission slip. Say no to dishes that only offer suffering. Say yes to complexity. To depth. To flavour that flirts instead of assaults. And if you ever find yourself tempted to dump chilli powder like it's confetti at a wedding, remember Tom. Think of his stew. Think of the neighbours.

CAROLINA REAPER
1,400 000 - 2,200 000
TRINIDAD SCORPION
1,200 000-2,000 000
GHOST PEPPER
855 000-1,041 427
HABANERO
100 000-350 000
CHOCOLATE HABANERO
SAVINA HABANERO
350000-577 000
SCOTCH BONNET
100 000-350 000
THAI
50 000-100 000
CAYENNE
30000-50000
SERRANO
10 000-23,000

3 UNDERSTANDING THE SCOVILLE SORCERY

You've stocked your pantry, met your chilli tribe, flirted with pastes, and hopefully learned not to set your guests' mouths on fire without a warning sign. Now we enter sacred territory. The chilli kingdom's royal ruler: The Scoville Scale. Equal parts genius and mischief, it's the chilli world's measuring stick, personality quiz, and safety manual, all rolled into one.

Think of the Scoville Scale as that brutally honest friend who tells you when your outfit is amazing and also when it looks like you lost a bet. It doesn't sugarcoat. It ranks heat in numbers, starting from the innocent bell pepper to the "why-would-you-do-this-to-yourself?" Carolina Reaper.

This chapter will pull back the curtain on what those numbers actually mean, how to read them without a chemistry degree, and how you can pair different heat levels with the right ingredients to create spicy harmony instead of kitchen chaos. We'll also uncover why some chillies feel fierce even with a lower Scoville rating, and which ones sneak up on you like a bad decision made after two margaritas.

By the end, you'll not only understand heat; you'll wield it. Like a kitchen sorcerer with a chilli wand and a mission.

How Hot Is Too Hot?

So now that we've met the majestic Scoville Scale, the next logical question is this: how hot is too hot? When does "just the right kick" become "I can see through time"?

Here's the thing. Heat tolerance isn't one-size-fits-all. What makes me sweat like a nervous politician at a live interview might be your idea of "mildly interesting." It's personal. It's biological. And sometimes, it's emotional.

Let me give you an example. A bloke named Steve—sweet, mild-mannered, looked like he played acoustic guitar in coffee shops—once boasted at a BBQ that "nothing's ever too hot for me." Classic last words. One chip with Carolina Reaper dust later, Steve was horizontal on a beanbag, breathing like he'd run a marathon through a sauna.

Now, was it funny? Yes. Did we check on him? Also yes. But here's the truth: spice is a spectrum. There's a fine line between adventurous heat and full-blown edible assault. You want excitement, not a visit from emergency services.

Scientifically speaking, your tongue is loaded with TRPV1 receptors, tiny heat-sensing gatekeepers that react to capsaicin, the compound responsible for chilli's kick (Caterina et al., 1997). The more capsaicin, the louder these receptors scream. And not everyone's receptors scream the same way. Some whisper. Some wail. Some perform dramatic operas.

Tolerance builds over time, just like strength at the gym. You wouldn't deadlift your own fridge on day one, right? Same rules apply. Start small. Get to know your limits. Learn to love the burn without becoming its victim.

And let's be honest, context matters too. Spicy food hits differently on a hot summer day versus a cold night with a glass of red wine. Your mood, metabolism, and what else you're eating all play a role. What's "too hot" on an empty stomach might feel like "just right" after a spoonful of creamy guac or a mouthful of rice.

Now, a practical tip I give all chilli-curious hosts: have cooling elements ready. Yoghurt dips. Fresh cucumber. Sweet chutneys. Creamy sauces. These don't just soothe the burn; they enhance the flavour. It's the contrast that makes spicy food magical. Heat alone is boring. Heat balanced is unforgettable.

Remember, the goal is pleasure, not punishment. If someone's face turns the colour of raw beetroot and they stop blinking, back off. No one wants a party guest passed out over a bowl of vindaloo.

The Scoville Scale Simplified

After watching poor Steve plead with the universe through pepper-induced tears, it's only fair that we now decode the spicy sorcery behind his downfall. Enter the Scoville Scale: part science, part black magic, part "what were you thinking?" warning label.

Let's keep it simple.

The Scoville Scale is like a chilli's brag sheet. It tells you how much capsaicin is present in the pepper. The higher the number, the more capsaicin. The more capsaicin, the more your mouth will feel like it licked a live wire during a thunderstorm.

Now, this scale wasn't invented by a modern spice wizard in a lab coat. No, it came from Wilbur Scoville, a cheerful American pharmacist who, in 1912, decided to measure chilli heat the same way some people test relationships: with dilution. He'd mix chilli extract into sugar water and feed it to volunteers (actual humans, bless them) until someone finally said, "Ah, I don't feel the burn anymore." The number of times it had to be diluted became the chilli's Scoville rating (Scoville, 1912). Imagine being that tester. "Still burning, Wilbur. Still burning…"

A bell pepper sits proudly at 0 Scoville Heat Units (SHU). Pure, innocent, incapable of betrayal. A jalapeño? Somewhere between 2,500 to 8,000 SHU. Mildly mischievous. Habaneros? A fiery leap to 100,000 to 350,000 SHU. And the infamous Carolina Reaper? Over 2 million SHU, which is basically "call your insurance provider first."

These days, scientists don't rely on poor interns sipping chilli juice. Instead, they use High-Performance Liquid Chromatography (HPLC), a fancy method that measures capsaicinoids more accurately (Govindarajan, 1986). But the old numbers stick around because, honestly, they sound way cooler.

But I hear you say, "Why does a jalapeño sometimes feel hotter than a habanero?" Excellent question. Factors like ripeness, where it was grown, and how it's cooked all mess with the heat. A jalapeño straight off the vine might pack more punch than a habanero that's been lounging in vinegar for weeks.

Here's what I do: I use the Scoville Scale as a guide, not gospel. It helps me know who I'm inviting to the dinner party and whether I should prep a yoghurt-based truce on the side.

You don't need to memorise the entire scale. Just remember the general vibe of each level and use it to choose wisely. Want a safe bet for mixed guests? Go for chillies under 30,000 SHU. Want to test your in-laws' loyalty? Bring out the habanero.

Pairing Heat with Ingredients

Alright, we've laughed at Steve, toasted Wilbur Scoville, and scaled the chilli ladder without losing a limb. But now comes the part where the real kitchen sorcery begins: pairing. Because let's face it: throwing chilli into a dish without understanding its co-stars is like casting Shakespeare with toddlers and hoping for *Macbeth*. Chaos. Improv. Possible fire.

Pairing heat isn't just about "Can I handle it?" It's about "Should I put this in here?" And the answer depends on who's on the plate with it. Chillies have personalities, and they either clash or dance depending on their partners.

Let's start with the love story: fat and heat. Butter, cream, coconut milk, cheese—they all take chilli by the hand and whisper, "Shhh… let's calm down." Fat absorbs capsaicin, softens its punch, and lets you taste the flavour without turning your tongue into a crime scene. That's why spicy curries go hand-in-hand with creamy yoghurt, and why hot wings pair like a dream with blue cheese dip.

Next up: sweet and heat. This is the couple who shouldn't work but somehow throw the best parties. Think mango and habanero. Honey and chipotle. Brown sugar with cayenne on roasted nuts. Sugar doesn't kill the heat, but it flirts with it. The contrast creates that addictive "ouch-but-wow" sensation that makes people come back for more even when they know better.

Then we've got acid and heat. Lime, vinegar, tomatoes. These cut through the richness and reset the palate. Acid sharpens everything, making the spice more vibrant and less one-dimensional. Add a squeeze of lime to your chilli stew and suddenly, it's singing soprano. Without acid, spice can feel like it's sitting in a hot bath with no exit. With it? Refreshing. Bold. Balanced.

Now let's talk carbs and heat. The unsung heroes. Bread, rice, noodles—they don't cool the heat, but they absorb it and spread it out. You ever notice how people don't scream as loudly when they eat spicy food wrapped in bread? That's not an accident. It's carb armour. Your mouth still burns, but it's manageable—like watching a horror film with your fingers half-covering your eyes.

If you're not sure what to do, try this rule: balance the burn with one soft, one sweet, or one sour. Add something that rounds it, lifts it, or neutralises it. Think cream with jalapeños. Pineapple with chillies. Lemon with harissa. Watch your dish go from "interesting" to "obsessed."

Sweet, Smoky, Tangy, or Fierce?

You've now earned your honorary chilli cape. You understand what heat is, how it plays, and which ingredients help keep it from staging a mouth mutiny. But we're not stopping there. Oh no. Because not all heat hits the same. Some sneak in like flirty troublemakers. Others kick the door down wearing steel boots and a salsa crown.

It's time to get acquainted with the flavour personalities of chilli. Because heat alone is boring. It's the personality behind the punch that makes a dish unforgettable. Let's talk through four of the boldest profiles: Sweet, Smoky, Tangy, and Fierce.

Sweet heat is the charmer. The chilli that hugs you before it slaps you. Habaneros are the poster child for this. Fruity, floral, warm like a tropical breeze... right before they start setting fires. That duality is delicious when paired with pineapple salsa, mango chutneys, or glazed meats. Sweet heat is what makes BBQ magic. It's also the reason people don't realise how hot it is until their upper lip is sweating and they've lost the ability to speak in full sentences.

Smoky heat is all drama and depth. We're talking chipotle, ancho, and smoked paprika. These chillies bring complexity. They're the jazz musicians of the spice world: smooth, moody, and a little mysterious. Perfect in stews, rubs, and anything you want to taste like it's been cooked over an open fire while someone told a ghost story. A friend once described chipotle chilli as "a campfire that flirted with bacon." I can't improve on that.

Then we've got **tangy heat**. These are the vinegar-forward chillies or dishes where acid is the frontman. Think pickled jalapeños, sambal oelek, and certain hot sauces like Louisiana-style or Peri-Peri. This type of heat dances on the tongue. It's zippy. Bright. The chilli version of someone who enters the party, hugs everyone, and still manages to steal the aux cord. Tangy heat is what you want on tacos, fried food, and dishes that need a jolt of wake-up flavour.

And finally... **fierce heat**. No-nonsense, breath-stealing, why-did-I-do-this-to-myself heat. This is where ghost peppers, Scotch bonnets, and Carolina Reapers roam. They don't pretend. They don't apologise. They're not here to enhance; they're here to dominate. These are the chillies for chilli-heads. For hot sauce collectors. For the slightly unhinged but endlessly entertaining. If sweet heat is a slow dance, fierce heat is a mosh pit in your mouth.

So, how do you choose which type to use? Ask yourself: what do I want this dish to *feel* like? Comforting? Go sweet and smoky. Refreshing? Try tangy. Ready to test someone's limits or create a meal that becomes legend (or lawsuit)? Bring the fierce.

And of course, there's nothing stopping you from mixing profiles. Some of the best hot sauces blend all four. That's when you create flavour that's layered, dynamic, and worth remembering. Because no one tells a story about the beige dip. But the one that was sweet, spicy, smoky, and left a slight tingle for three hours? That one makes it into group chats.

4 SMALL BITES THAT PACK A PUNCH

You've braved the Scoville sorcery, matched heat with flavour like a culinary composer, and probably questioned your life choices somewhere between "mildly zingy" and "where's the milk?" But now, we're heading into the party zone: appetisers, finger foods, and cheeky little bites that wear chilli like a pair of red stilettos. Not overdone. Not desperate. Just enough to turn heads.

Because here's the thing: the opening act of any good gathering isn't the main dish; it's the small bites. These little legends set the tone. They say, "Yes, I came to entertain," without making anyone feel like they need to sign a waiver. And chillies? They belong right here. In snacks that surprise. In dips that whisper danger. In canapés that disappear faster than secrets at a hen night.

This chapter is about building flavour bombs in tiny portions. We'll cover how to make fiery finger food that people can actually eat while standing. We'll play with dips, spreads, and a few spicy twists on familiar favourites. And we'll keep it all delicious, doable, and crowd-approved.

Because let's be honest: if you can make your guests sweat before the main course, and they still beg for more? You, my friend, are already winning.

Spicy Canapés and Bold Bites

Now, I know what you're thinking. "Canapés? Sounds fancy. Sounds fiddly. Sounds like something that involves tweezers and caviar and a mortgage extension." But hear me out. Canapés don't have to be fussy. They just have to be fabulous. And when you add a little chilli? Darling, they don't just enter the room; they strut.

Let's start with a truth I live by: people love small food. There's something about a bite-sized snack that feels indulgent. You can eat six of them and still claim you're "just nibbling." Add heat to that equation, and you've got something memorable. Something that whispers on first bite, then throws a punch with a smile.

A friend of mine, Liv, once brought jalapeño and cream cheese-stuffed dates wrapped in bacon to a New Year's party. Tiny. Inoffensive-looking. Barely needed cutlery. People ate them like popcorn, until the warmth crept in. Then came the collective gasp. Followed by the applause. Liv has since been promoted to Head of Party Snacks in her friendship group. She's never allowed to show up without those dates again.

Here are three spicy canapés that never fail me:

MINI SPICY TOSTADAS

CRUNCHY, CREAMY, AND SWEET WITH A FIERY FINISH.

YIELD: MAKES 20-24 BITES **HEAT LEVEL: 🌶🌶 (MEDIUM)**

INGREDIENTS:

- bag of bite-sized tortilla chips or plantain chips
- 1 cup guacamole
- 1 cup spicy black bean puree (see Pro Tip below)
- 1/2 cup crumbled feta cheese
- 1/4 cup habanero mango salsa

METHOD:

1. Lay the bite-sized chips out on a serving platter.
2. Top each chip first with a small spoonful of guacamole, then a dollop of spicy black bean puree.
3. Sprinkle with crumbled feta and finish with a tiny dot of habanero mango salsa.
4. Serve immediately.

CHILLI-CRUSTED HALLOUMI CUBES

SALTY, SQUEAKY, SPICY HEAVEN.

YIELD: MAKES 20-24 BITES

HEAT LEVEL: 🌶🌶 (MEDIUM)

INGREDIENTS:

- 1 block (225g) halloumi cheese, diced into 2cm cubes
- 1 tbsp smoked paprika
- 1 tsp crushed chilli flakes
- 1 tsp honey
- 1 tbsp olive oil
- For the dip: 1/2 cup Greek yoghurt, juice of 1/2 lime, 1 tbsp chopped fresh coriander or mint

METHOD:

1. In a bowl, toss the halloumi cubes with smoked paprika, chilli flakes, honey, and olive oil until evenly coated.

2. Heat a non-stick pan over medium-high heat. Sear the halloumi cubes for 1-2 minutes on each side, until golden brown and crispy.

3. While the halloumi is cooking, mix the Greek yoghurt, lime juice, and fresh herbs in a small bowl to create the dip.

4. Serve the hot halloumi cubes with the yoghurt-lime dip on the side for dipping.

BLISTERED SHISHITO PEPPERS

EDIBLE ROULETTE WHERE ONE IN TEN IS A SPICY SURPRISE

YIELD: SERVES 4 AS A SNACK **HEAT LEVEL: (MILD, WITH A CHANCE OF)**

INGREDIENTS:

- 225g shishito peppers
- 1 tbsp vegetable or avocado oil
- Flaky sea salt
- 1 lime, cut into wedges

METHOD:

1. Toss the shishito peppers in the oil until lightly coated.

2. Heat a large skillet or wok over high heat. Add the peppers in a single layer (you may need to do this in batches).

3. Cook, turning occasionally, for 5-7 minutes until the peppers are blistered and charred in spots.

4. Transfer to a serving plate, sprinkle generously with flaky sea salt, and serve immediately with lime wedges for squeezing over.

Want to go extra cheeky? Make a "Russian Roulette Platter": nine mild bites, one scorcher. Let your guests play with fate. Just warn them first, or at least keep napkins and a dairy-based drink nearby. You don't want anyone snorting soda from surprise.

The beauty of spicy canapés is that they wake up the palate. They get people talking. They loosen tension and replace it with happy snacking and little waves of warmth. You're not trying to burn mouths here. You're trying to start a slow dance with the taste buds.

And you don't need a full catering setup. Use what you've got. Mini skewers. Toothpicks. Tiny bowls. Even shot glasses. Yes, shot glasses—perfect for spicy gazpacho shooters with a sliver of pickled chilli on top. It's like a spa treatment for spice lovers.

According to food researchers Tan and Lee (2017), chilli-based snacks can actually stimulate appetite and boost social engagement. Which makes sense. Nothing gets a room talking like a shared "Wait… is this spicy to you?" moment.

Now take something like halloumi. It's salty. It squeaks. It's cheese that somehow grills like steak. Add a smoky chilli crust and suddenly, you've turned science into snack magic. (Don't just take my word for it; McGee's *On Food and Cooking* (2004) explains how protein structure in cheeses like halloumi resists melting, making it perfect for spicy grilling.).

And if you've ever wondered why people reach for more despite the burn, blame your brain. Researchers Prescott and Stevenson (1996) found that our brains often associate spicy foods with reward and pleasure, especially in social settings. It's like our nervous system yells "Danger!" while our dopamine whispers, "Do it again."

The Art of Fiery Dips & Spreads

Every dinner party has that one moment.
The music's good. The drinks are flowing. People are mingling, eyes darting to the table like wolves in casual wear. And then… someone spots it. The bowl. No label. No warning. Just a creamy-looking dip, smooth and glistening, sitting between the carrot sticks like it's done nothing wrong.

They dip.

They chew.

They pause.

Then come the four fateful words:

"What is in this?"

That, my friend, is the power of a fiery dip. It lures you in with softness, with beauty, with garlic and lime and maybe a touch of yoghurt. But under the surface? Heat. Purposeful heat. The kind that builds like a drumroll. Not an explosion. A seduction.

See, dips and spreads are dangerous in the best way. They pretend to be the sidekick, but they often steal the entire show. Scientists like Shepherd (2006) have pointed out that flavour is a multisensory illusion. You don't just taste it. You smell it. Feel it. Even hear it crunch on a chip. So when you marry that sensory orchestra with chilli? You don't get a condiment. You get a statement.

And oh, the variety.

HARISSA LABNEH

CREAMY, COOL, AND KICKED BY NORTH AFRICAN FIRE

YIELD: SERVES 6-8 **HEAT LEVEL: 🌶🌶 (MEDIUM)**

INGREDIENTS:

- 2 cups labneh (or thick Greek yoghurt)
- 2-3 tbsp harissa paste (adjust to taste)
- 1 tsp ground cumin
- Salt to taste
- Optional garnish: drizzle of olive oil, chopped coriander (skip if your guests are anti-coriander)

METHOD:

1. In a medium bowl, combine the labneh, harissa paste, cumin, and salt. Stir until well combined and swirled.

2. Transfer to a serving bowl. Drizzle with olive oil and garnish with chopped coriander if using.

3. Serve with crackers, flatbread, or vegetable crudités.

SPICY MUHAMMARA

A SMOKY, SWEET, AND NUTTY DIP WITH A SLOW-BUILDING WARMTH.

YIELD: SERVES 6-8 **HEAT LEVEL: (MEDIUM)**

INGREDIENTS:

- 2 large red bell peppers, roasted, peeled, and deseeded
- 1 cup walnuts, toasted
- 2 tbsp pomegranate molasses
- 1 tbsp Aleppo pepper flakes (or 1 tsp crushed chilli flakes)
- 1/2 cup breadcrumbs
- 1 garlic clove, minced
- 1/2 tsp ground cumin
- 1/4 cup olive oil, plus more for drizzling
- Salt to taste

METHOD:

1. Place all ingredients except the olive oil into a food processor. Pulse until roughly combined.

2. With the processor running, slowly stream in the olive oil until the dip is cohesive but still has some texture.

3. Season with salt to taste. Transfer to a bowl, drizzle with more olive oil, and serve

Want drama? Mix chipotle in adobo with cream cheese and lime. Serve cold. Watch your friends question what they just experienced. Then serve it again and watch them pretend they were ready this time. Researchers Tan and Lee (2017) call this repeat-spice behaviour "hedonic resilience." I call it "proof your dip just won."

The trick with spicy dips is in balance and texture. A too-thin dip feels like punishment. A too-thick one clogs the moment. Aim for silky, bold, and layered. Let the heat bloom, not blind.

And don't you dare serve just one. Offer a trio. Mild, medium, fierce. Line them up like a dare. I promise, even your spice-shy guests will tiptoe toward the hot end by the third cracker. Because they're human. And humans are curious, chaotic little creatures.

Chilli-Infused Cheese Boards

So, we've smeared our dips, passed out napkins for those who underestimated the "medium" bowl, and watched guests fall in love with muhammara like it was a long-lost summer fling. But now it's time to crank the charm up.
You know where I'm going, don't you? Cheese. Glorious, gooey, glorious cheese. But not just any cheese. We're talking chilli-infused, spice-kissed, dangerously addictive cheese boards that walk the fine line between elegance and full-blown obsession.

Let me put it this way: if regular cheese boards whisper class, a chilli cheese board kicks open the door in leather boots and pours wine before anyone's asked. It's exciting. It's unexpected. It tells your guests, "Yes, I own a cheese knife... and yes, it's been near jalapeños."

Now here's what I know:

The human brain responds to cheese and spice together in a way that borders on euphoric. The creaminess of the cheese helps buffer the burn, while the spice gives the cheese a bit of sass it didn't know it needed. According to Drewnowski and Gomez-Carneros (2000), fatty foods like cheese activate pleasure centres in the brain, and when you add spice, you double the drama and the dopamine.

I once went to a wine and cheese night hosted by a woman named Ursula. Sounds posh already, right? Wrong. She brought a chilli jam so good it almost caused a riot. Picture aged cheddar, barely crumbly, stacked with a spoonful of this deep red chilli-laced magic. People stopped speaking. One guy made a sound like he'd just seen the Northern Lights. Ursula's chilli jam became legendary. No one remembers the brie. Everyone remembers that.

So, what belongs on a chilli-forward cheese board?
Start with cheeses that can handle heat. Aged cheddar. Manchego. Gouda.

Even a bold blue cheese, if your guests are the adventurous type. Then bring in the chilli elements:

- Chilli jams and chutneys – sweet, sticky, with a background of fire.
- Candied jalapeños – like little spicy gummy bears that went to finishing school.
- Chilli-spiced nuts or seeds – crunch with a warning label.
- Smoked meats with a pepper kick – think soppressata or chorizo with chilli flakes tucked in like spicy secrets.

Want a shortcut to looking brilliant? Sprinkle smoked paprika over whipped ricotta. Serve with crackers. Watch people assume you've been trained by a culinary wizard.

Texture matters too. Pair soft cheeses with crunchy elements. Use toasted bread, seedy crackers, pickled chillies for acidity. A great board plays with contrast like a jazz band plays with rhythm: wild but intentional.

And the visuals? Stunning. Red against cream. Green chillies sliced into rings. Golden crackers. Your board doesn't just feed the stomach. It seduces the eye.

Jalapeño Poppers, Reimagined

Cheese boards? Handled. Dips? Dangerous in the best way. Guests? Properly warmed up and circling the snack table like curious cats. But now… now we reach the crowd-pleaser. The party MVP. The small-but-mighty legend that turns even the chilli-hesitant into repeat offenders: the jalapeño popper.

But not just any popper. We're reinventing it. No more sad, soggy supermarket versions that taste like disappointment wrapped in breadcrumbs. No more over-fried cheese grenades that explode in your mouth with the subtlety of a firecracker in a shoebox.

This section is about elevating the popper. Keeping the soul, but adding the sass. And I promise, you won't need a culinary degree or twelve gadgets. Just some jalapeños, a little creativity, and the willingness to be crowned Host of the Year.

First, a bit of context. Jalapeños clock in at 2,500–8,000 Scoville Heat Units, according to Bosland and Votava (2012). That's just enough heat to tease, not terrify. And they're structurally perfect for stuffing. Like nature designed them for drama.

Now, the classic version is simple: halve the jalapeños, scoop out the seeds, fill with cream cheese, wrap in bacon, bake. Boom. You've got yourself a tray of spicy little gifts. But you didn't come here for ordinary.

Let's remix.

THE FANCY POPPER

BLUE CHEESE, CARAMELISED ONION, AND WALNUT SOPHISTICATION

YIELD: MAKES 20 POPPERS **HEAT LEVEL: (MEDIUM)**

INGREDIENTS:

- 10 large fresh jalapeños, halved lengthwise and deseeded
- 1 package (225g) cream cheese, softened
- 2 tbsp roasted garlic paste
- 1/4 cup caramelised onions, finely chopped
- 1/4 cup crumbled blue cheese
- 1/4 cup walnuts, finely chopped

METHOD:

1. Preheat oven to 200°C (400°F). Line a baking sheet with parchment paper.

2. In a bowl, mix the cream cheese, roasted garlic, caramelised onions, and blue cheese until well combined.

3. Spoon the mixture into the jalapeño halves, filling them generously.

4. Sprinkle the chopped walnuts over the top of each stuffed popper.

5. Bake for 18-20 minutes, until the jalapeños are tender and the filling is bubbly.

THE GLOBAL POPPER

A FLAVOUR TRIP WITH TIKKA MASALA AND PANEER.

YIELD: MAKES 20 POPPERS **HEAT LEVEL: 🌶🌶 (MEDIUM)**

INGREDIENTS:

- 10 large fresh jalapeños, halved lengthwise and deseeded
- 1 package (225g) cream cheese, softened
- 2 tbsp tikka masala paste
- 2 tbsp fresh coriander, chopped
- 1/2 cup paneer, grated or crumbled
- For serving: mint yoghurt

METHOD:

1. Preheat oven to 200°C (400°F). Line a baking sheet with parchment paper.

2. In a bowl, mix the cream cheese, tikka masala paste, and coriander until combined.

3. Spoon the mixture into the jalapeño halves. Top generously with the paneer.

4. Bake for 18-20 minutes, until the paneer is lightly golden.

5. Serve warm with a side of mint yoghurt for dipping.

THE SWEET-HOT SURPRISE

MASCARPONE, HONEY, AND GINGER WRAPPED IN PROSCIUTTO

YIELD: MAKES 20 POPPERS **HEAT LEVEL:) (MILD)**

INGREDIENTS:

- 10 large fresh jalapeños, halved lengthwise and deseeded
- 1 cup mascarpone cheese
- 1 tbsp honey
- 2 tbsp candied ginger, finely diced
- 10 slices prosciutto, cut in half
- For serving: hot honey for drizzling

METHOD:

1. Preheat oven to 200°C (400°F). Line a baking sheet with parchment paper.
2. In a bowl, mix the mascarpone, honey, and candied ginger.
3. Spoon the mixture into the jalapeño halves.
4. Wrap each stuffed jalapeño half with a half-slice of prosciutto.
5. Bake for 15-18 minutes, until the prosciutto is crisp at the edges.
6. Drizzle with hot honey before serving

What makes poppers irresistible is the combo of texture, temperature, and taste. The crunch of the pepper, the softness of the filling, the rising warmth in the mouth—it's a story in a bite. And according to Kinnamon (2012), this kind of multi-sensory eating actually enhances flavour perception and makes food more memorable. People talk about these things, you know. I once heard a man at a garden party casually say, "Remember Sharon's poppers from last year?" Sharon didn't even host that year. That's the power of a good popper. They linger in memory like exes with great playlists.

Tips for perfecting your popper game:

- Always de-seed. Unless you're hosting a chilli initiation ritual, take out the heat core.
- Don't overfill. Melted cheese lava is fun until it fuses to your baking tray like emotional baggage.
- Balance the flavours. Creamy + spicy + crunchy + optional sweet = applause.

5 SAUCERY & MARINADE MAGIC

Well, look at you, still here, still curious, and hopefully still recovering from those legendary poppers.

Welcome to Chapter 5, my flavour-hunting, heat-loving comrade. First, let me just say: thank you. You've made it through chilli-infused cheese boards, suspicious dips, flavour flirting, jalapeño roulette, and a whole parade of ingredients with attitude. That takes stamina, courage, and a digestive tract worthy of knighthood.

Now, before we march into marinade territory, let's take a quick breath. Think back. Remember when we were shyly talking about bell peppers in Chapter 2, like nervous guests at a school dance? And now? Now you're pairing habaneros with mango like a flavour alchemist in a salsa lab. Growth. Pure growth.

But here's the thing: we've only scratched the surface of what chillies can do. Because when you mix them into sauces and marinades? You don't just add heat; you build worlds. A good sauce doesn't sit on the plate. It walks into the room, claps its hands, and makes everything else taste like it finally found its purpose.

This chapter is where the sorcery begins. Liquid fire, silky glazes, sticky rubs that turn meat, tofu, veg, and even spoons into experiences worth remembering.

Building Layers of Heat

If you thought jalapeño poppers were spicy foreplay, welcome to the full moon ritual. This is where we stop flirting with chilli and start building relationships—messy, intense, flavour-rich relationships. Because sauce? Sauce isn't a topping. It's not an afterthought. A good sauce builds tension. It seduces the tongue. It escalates drama with every bite.

But hold on. Don't confuse "building heat" with just chucking more chillies into the pot like you're punishing your enemies. No, no. That's what amateurs do. What we're doing here? This is saucery. This is slow, purposeful, step-by-step heat architecture. We're not lighting a fire. We're crafting an inferno with nuance.

Let me tell you a story.

There's a guy I know, Matt. Lovely bloke. Obsessed with barbecues. One day, he proudly invites the gang over to try his "secret hot sauce" he'd been fermenting for three weeks in a dark cupboard like a potion. The result? Carnage. One spoonful and my friend Kelly started sweating from her ankles. Another guest quietly left and returned with an ice pack and existential dread. The flavour? Nonexistent. It was just pain. Like licking a chainsaw mid-revolution.

Matt's mistake? No layering. No softness before the storm. Just raw, unrefined rage in a bottle.

You? You're going to do better.

Here's how you build proper heat, layer by layer.

Step 1: Start with aromatics.

Onions. Garlic. Ginger. Chillies love to party with these guys. They open up the dish, create the base, and make everything smell like you know what you're doing, even if you're making it up as you go. According to McGee (2004), garlic and onion compounds enhance the perceived heat in a dish by stimulating similar receptors. Translation? They set the stage for spice to shine.

Step 2: Toast your spice.

Before you even think about the sauce, toast your dry spices: paprika, cumin, chilli powder. This unlocks their oils and gives you warmth instead of bitterness. Think of it like stretching before a workout. Skip it, and you're just risking injury to your tongue's trust.

Step 3: Use chilli at multiple points.

Add some at the beginning for depth. A little in the middle for build. Then maybe a finishing touch: a swirl of hot oil, a chopped fresh chilli, or a drizzle of fermented sauce for that final kick. Bosland and Baral (2007) explain that layering capsaicinoids creates a longer-lasting, fuller heat experience instead of a single spike of pain.

Step 4: Balance it. Always.

Add sweet (honey, maple, brown sugar), acid (vinegar, lime), or fat (butter, coconut milk). This keeps your sauce from becoming a weapon. You want people to fear your sauce a little, but also love it. Like an ex who sends really good memes.

Real-life example?

I once made a spicy pineapple glaze for grilled prawns using fresh chilli, ginger, lime, and a splash of dark rum. It started sweet. Mellow. Then… heat. Not slap-you heat. Slow heat. The kind that crept up like a bad idea on a good night. People didn't just eat it; they talked about it. They asked for jars. One guy proposed. I said no, but still, impact.

This is your power now. You're not just making sauce. You're crafting narrative. Every bite should have a beginning, middle, and dramatic spicy finale.

Sauces That Seduce (and Bite Back)

If the last section taught us how to build heat like an architect with a grudge, then this one? This is about what happens when that heat takes off its glasses, puts on red lipstick, and enters the room to ruin you, in a good way.

Sauces are not background singers. They're not wallflowers. A good sauce doesn't wait politely to be noticed. It walks straight up to the dish and makes it better-looking. And when that sauce has chilli in it? That's a game-changer.

Let's get one thing straight: I'm not talking about the mass-produced, vinegar-flavoured chaos that tries to melt your face off for fun. No, we're talking flavour-forward sauces. The kind that whisper before they roar. That seduce the taste buds with citrus, garlic, herbs, or a sneaky splash of something fermented, then remind you who's boss with a warm, cheeky sting.

According to Shepherd (2006), what makes a sauce memorable isn't just the heat; it's the way our brain interprets smell and taste together. That's why a chilli-lime sauce smells sexy before you even taste it, and why roasted garlic with chipotle feels like a warm hug… with an electric jolt on the end.

Let me paint you a picture.

A friend of mine, Hannah, once hosted a "wings and wine" night. Casual vibe. Until she brought out her homemade sticky chilli-garlic glaze. It looked innocent enough: deep red, glossy, fragrant. But one bite in and the room changed. Eyes widened. One guy made a sound I can only describe as "emotional damage in falsetto." Another guest asked, dead serious, "Is this what happiness tastes like?"

That sauce? It balanced. It bit, yes, but it also had sweetness, acidity, umami. According to McGee (2004), these contrasts activate multiple taste pathways, keeping the brain engaged and the fork moving back in for more.

So, what makes a great seductress of a sauce?

Start with a base: roasted tomatoes, garlic, or miso. Add your heat element: fresh chillies, fermented pastes, or infused oils. Now soften it: maybe honey, mango, or brown sugar. Next, spike it with acid: lemon juice, vinegar, tamarind. Finally, hit it with umami: soy, fish sauce, or anchovy paste. That complexity? That's the difference between a date and a situation.

Want your sauce to bite back? Use fermented ingredients. A little funk goes a long way. According to Tamang et al. (2016), fermentation boosts both flavour and digestibility. Your sauce gains depth, your gut gets a hug, and your guests get addicted.

Try a smoky tamarind chilli glaze for ribs. Or a fermented chilli peanut sauce over noodles. Or my personal favourite, scotch bonnet, mango, lime juice, and a dash of Caribbean curry powder. Put that on roast chicken and prepare for applause. Possibly tears.

Just remember: a sauce should support the dish, not steal the spotlight entirely. It should elevate, not dominate. Think partner, not dictator.

DIY Peri-Peri, Harissa & Gochujang

So, we've officially entered saucy territory, the kind where dinner guests fall silent, then slowly exhale words like "wow" and "I need this bottled." We've already talked about sauces that seduce. Now let's talk about cult classics. The sauces with street cred. The flavour powerhouses. The ones with accents, passports, and stories.

I'm talking about Peri-Peri, Harissa, and Gochujang.

Each one comes from a different corner of the world, and each one punches with its own rhythm. If sauces were music, Peri-Peri would be Afrobeat with a citrus twist. Harissa? Smoky North African jazz with heavy drums. Gochujang? Fermented Korean funk that gets better the longer you listen. Or in this case, taste.

Let's break them down.

DIY PERI-PERI SAUCE

ZESTY, FIERY, AND VIBRANT AFRO-PORTUGUESE GLORY.

YIELD: MAKES ABOUT 1 CUP **HEAT LEVEL:))) (HOT)**

INGREDIENTS:

- 10-12 African bird's eye chillies (or Thai chillies), stems removed
- 4 cloves garlic, peeled
- 1/2 cup olive oil
- 1/4 cup red wine vinegar
- Juice of 1 lemon
- 1 tsp smoked paprika
- 1/2 tsp salt

METHOD:

1. Combine all ingredients in a blender or food processor.
2. Blend until a coarse or smooth paste forms, depending on your preference.
3. Transfer to a jar and let it sit for at least a few hours, preferably overnight, for the flavours to meld.
4. Use as a marinade for chicken or prawns, or as a fiery table sauce.

DIY HARISSA PASTE

THE SMOKY, DEEP, AND FLORAL QUEEN OF NORTH AFRICA

YIELD: MAKES ABOUT 3/4 CUP **HEAT LEVEL: 🌶🌶 (MEDIUM)**

INGREDIENTS:

- 4-5 dried guajillo or ancho chillies
- 2 dried red chillies (for heat, e.g., de arbol)
- 2 cloves garlic
- 1 tsp ground coriander
- 1 tsp ground caraway seeds
- 1/2 tsp ground cumin
- 3 tbsp olive oil, plus more for storing
- 1 tbsp tomato paste
- Salt to taste

METHOD:

1. Remove the stems and seeds from the dried chillies. Place them in a bowl and cover with boiling water. Let soak for 30 minutes until softened. Drain, reserving a few tablespoons of the soaking liquid.

2. In a dry pan, toast the coriander, caraway, and cumin for 1 minute until fragrant.

3. Combine the soaked chillies, toasted spices, garlic, tomato paste, and 3 tbsp olive oil in a blender. Blend, adding a spoonful of the soaking water if needed, until a smooth paste forms.

4. Season with salt. Store in a jar, covered with a layer of olive oil

DIY GOCHUJANG-STYLE GLAZE

A QUICK, FERMENTED-FUNKY, SWEET-AND-SPICY KOREAN-INSPIRED GLAZE.

YIELD: MAKES ABOUT 1 CUP **HEAT LEVEL: (MEDIUM)**

INGREDIENTS:

- 1/4 cup gochujang paste
- 2 tbsp soy sauce (or tamari)
- 2 tbsp rice vinegar
- 1 tbsp sesame oil
- 1 tbsp honey or maple syrup
- 2 cloves garlic, minced
- 1 tsp fresh ginger, grated

METHOD:

1. Whisk all ingredients together in a small saucepan until smooth.
2. Heat over low, stirring constantly, for 3-4 minutes until warmed through and slightly thickened.
3. Use as a glaze for grilled meats, tofu, or eggplant, or as a dipping sauce.

Peri-Peri (also spelled piri-piri or pili-pili, because even the spelling wants options) is a zesty chilli sauce from Mozambique by way of Portugal, now a global flame thrower thanks to chains like Nando's. At its core: African bird's eye chillies, garlic, vinegar, lemon juice, and oil. What makes it glorious is that layered acidity. According to Bosland and Votava (2012), vinegar not only sharpens the heat but helps preserve and amplify flavour, especially when mixed with oil-based ingredients.

Harissa, born in Tunisia and now a staple across North Africa and the Middle East, is deep, smoky, rich, and intense. It doesn't slap you like Peri-Peri. It smoulders. Made with roasted red peppers, garlic, coriander, caraway, cumin, and dried chillies, it adds mystery to everything from stews to sandwiches.

One friend of mine once slathered homemade Harissa on a burger and got a standing ovation from her in-laws. This is a woman who once burned toast in a microwave. That's Harissa power. As McGee (2004) explains, spice and aroma-rich foods like these stimulate not just the taste buds, but the olfactory system, creating a fuller sensory experience.

Gochujang is the thick, sweet-salty, fermented chilli paste that's been a backbone of Korean cooking for over 1,000 years. It's made with glutinous rice, fermented soybeans, red chilli powder, and salt, and it's as bold as it sounds. Fermented foods like gochujang don't just add heat. They bring umami. Depth. The kind of funk that makes bland food run away crying. Tamang et al. (2016) noted that gochujang's fermentation process increases bioavailability of nutrients and gut health. So yes, gochujang makes you cooler and healthier. Miracle in a jar.

If you don't have time to ferment your own (because you're not a wizard monk living on a chilli farm), buy good-quality paste and stir it into mayo, stews, or marinades for instant soul.

Real-life tip: Mix gochujang with maple syrup and soy sauce. Brush it on grilled eggplant. You'll eat it. You'll cry. You'll text people about it.

These sauces aren't just spicy. They're cultural events. They carry legacy, boldness, and unapologetic flavour. When you make or use them, you're not just cooking; you're travelling without leaving the kitchen.

Spice Mixes for Every Occasion

Alright, you spicy legend. Let's be honest. We've been flying high on sauce glory. We've rubbed shoulders with fermented Korean royalty, spooned fire-roasted harissa onto burgers, and flirted shamelessly with zesty Peri-Peri. But now we're talking about spice mixes, and if that makes you yawn, hold your cinnamon stick right there.

This is not the bit where we talk about dusty jars from 2004 that live at the back of the pantry next to a packet of forgotten quinoa. This is where we make magic dust. Potions. Flavour spells. The kind of blends that make your oven smell like a Moroccan spice market at sunrise or a southern BBQ at full swagger.

Here's the truth: a good spice mix doesn't just season food. It changes identity. You're not making chicken. You're making jerk chicken with a backstory. You're not roasting potatoes. You're summoning crispy little devils coated in smoked paprika and thyme that make people fight over the last one.

Let me give you the real-world proof. I once handed my friend Charli a small jar of homemade Berbere, an Ethiopian blend packed with chilli, fenugreek, ginger, cinnamon, and clove. She sprinkled it on roasted carrots and brought them to a dinner party. No one touched the beef. They just ate carrots and asked for the recipe like they were collecting Pokémon cards. One guy took a photo of the spice jar. Just the jar. That's how deep it went.

Here's why spice blends matter:

When you mix spices, they stop shouting individual names and start singing harmonies. McGee (2004) notes that many spices share overlapping aroma compounds; when paired intentionally, they create an enhanced synergy of flavour that a single spice can't replicate. It's like having a band instead of a solo kazoo.

Let's get to the goods. Here are 4 bold spice blends you should know, use, and possibly whisper sweet nothings to while cooking:

BERBERE SPICE BLEND

ETHIOPIA'S COMPLEX AND WARMING DRAMA QUEEN

YIELD: MAKES ABOUT 1/2 CUP **HEAT LEVEL:))) (HOT)**

INGREDIENTS:

- 2 tbsp chilli flakes
- 2 tbsp paprika
- 1 tbsp ground ginger
- 2 tsp ground cinnamon
- 1 tsp ground cloves
- 1 tsp ground fenugreek
- 1 tsp ground cardamom
- 1 tsp black pepper

METHOD:

1. Combine all spices in a bowl and whisk thoroughly, or grind together in a spice grinder for a finer powder.

2. Store in an airtight jar away from light and heat. Use on lentils, roasted vegetables, or lamb.

SHATTA DUST

A MIDDLE EASTERN FIRECRACKER OF PURE CHILLI ENERGY

YIELD: MAKES ABOUT 1/3 CUP **HEAT LEVEL:))) (HOT)**

INGREDIENTS:

- 1/2 cup crushed dried chillies (e.g., cayenne or bird's eye)
- 1 tbsp garlic powder
- 2 tsp ground cumin
- 1 tsp dried mint
- Zest of one lemon, dried

METHOD:

1. Combine all ingredients in a spice grinder and pulse until you achieve a coarse or fine powder, as desired.

2. Store in an airtight jar. Sprinkle over hummus, grilled chicken, or pizza.

SMOKY BBQ RUB

THE NO-EXPLANATION-NEEDED CLASSIC FOR RIBS AND MORE.

YIELD: MAKES ABOUT 3/4 CUP **HEAT LEVEL: 🌶🌶 (MEDIUM)**

INGREDIENTS:

- 3 tbsp smoked paprika
- 2 tbsp brown sugar
- 1 tbsp cayenne pepper
- 1 tbsp garlic powder
- 1 tbsp black pepper
- 1 tbsp salt

METHOD:

1. Mix all ingredients thoroughly in a bowl.

2. Store in an airtight jar. Rub generously on ribs, chicken, or use to season roasted sweet potato fries.

CHEEKY CURRY MIX

AN INDIAN-ISH, BOLD, AND FAST BLEND FOR WEEKNIGHT WINS.

YIELD: MAKES ABOUT 1/2 CUP **HEAT LEVEL: 🌶🌶 (MEDIUM)**

INGREDIENTS:

- 2 tbsp turmeric
- 2 tbsp ground cumin
- 2 tbsp ground coriander
- 1 tbsp Kashmiri chilli powder (or 2 tsp paprika + 1 tsp cayenne)
- 1 tbsp garam masala
- 1 tsp ground fennel

METHOD:

1. Whisk all spices together until uniformly combined.

2. Store in an airtight jar. Use as a dry rub, or fry in oil to start a killer curry.

And don't forget: grind fresh when you can. Toast whole spices in a dry pan. Smell the release. Feel the flavour come alive. According to Stevenson (2009), freshly ground spices release volatile oils that degrade quickly, meaning your food tastes exponentially better when you ditch the stale stuff.

Make it personal. Mix in crushed dried herbs, lemon powder, or even a pinch of brown sugar. Make a batch. Jar it. Label it with something cheeky like "Potion #7" or "Rub Me Right." It'll become your secret weapon.

6 HOT MAINS FOR BRAVE GUESTS

You've seasoned. You've sauced. You've sprinkled magic powders like a chilli-fuelled wizard with a grudge and a measuring spoon. But now, it's time to bring the heat home. This chapter isn't about teasing. It's not about flirting with fire. This is the main event. The headline act. The dish that walks onto the table, cracks its knuckles, and says, "Let's see who's brave."

Welcome to Hot Mains for Brave Guests, a chapter dedicated to the bold, the curious, and the downright reckless. These aren't your average Tuesday-night meals. These are the dishes that make people sweat, grin, and unbutton their collars by bite three. But, and this is important, they're not just hot for hot's sake. No chilli chest-thumping here. We're talking flavour-forward fire, where the heat elevates the dish instead of hijacking it.

Because the goal isn't to send your guests into hiding. The goal is to make them fall in love. Bite by bite. Flame by flame.

Whether it's bold barbecues, chilli-drenched comfort food, or stews that whisper warnings with every spoonful, this chapter is your playground. Aprons on. Mouths ready. Courage advisable.

Bold Barbecues: Smoke Meets Fire

Alright, grab your tongs and your bravado, because this is not the chapter for the faint of taste buds. This is where smoke flirts with fire, where meat turns into legend, and where marinades hum lullabies before setting your tongue on a slow, sultry blaze. This, my friend, is barbecue with bite.

Now, I'm not talking about your uncle's "burn it 'til it's safe" sausages. I'm talking about bold barbecue, rubs that smack, sauces that seduce, and grill lines that deserve their own modelling contract. This is the kind of food that makes neighbours sniff the air and silently question their own life choices.

Let me tell you about Jerome.

Jerome hosted a summer cookout every year. Burgers, beers, vibes, great guy. But one year, he got cocky. He slathered store-bought ghost pepper sauce on his ribs and bragged that "only real men could handle it." Three bites in, Jerome was shirtless, chugging milk straight from the carton, eyes wide like he'd seen the afterlife.

Lesson? Don't mistake pure pain for proper BBQ heat. Great barbecue balances smoke, char, fat, and fire. And it builds flavour like a great novel, slowly, with twists.

The Foundations of Fiery Barbecue:

1. Dry Rub = Personality

Start with a smoky base: smoked paprika, garlic powder, cumin. Add heat: cayenne, black pepper, ground chipotle. Sweeten it: brown sugar or coconut sugar. Salt it generously. This creates a crust, a bark, that tastes like the crunchy climax of a suspense novel.
According to McGee (2004), the Maillard reaction (that gorgeous browning magic) hits harder when sugars and proteins mingle over high heat. So yes, your dry rub is science with seasoning.

2. Marinades = Seduction

Want meat that's bold but tender? Mix chillies with acid (lime, vinegar), fat (oil, yoghurt), and aromatics (onion, garlic, ginger). Let it sit. Let it think about its life. Let it soak in your spicy intentions.
A study by Tamang et al. (2016) found that acid and fermentation (like yoghurt or lime juice) break down muscle fibres, tenderising meat while enhancing chilli absorption. Translation: flavour that hits deeper, lasts longer.

3. The Grill = Theatre

Grill over indirect heat, then finish over flame for char. Keep a spray bottle of diluted apple juice or vinegar to mist the meat; it adds moisture and keeps your fire from throwing tantrums. That smokiness? That's nature's cologne.
And don't stop at meat. Grilled pineapple with chilli-honey glaze, eggplant with harissa rub, or portobellos with gochujang butter can outshine your steaks if you do it right. Fire is not exclusive. It's a generous lover.

4. The Sauce = Curtain Call

Brush on your sauce at the end, not the beginning. Otherwise, it burns before it blesses. Try a mix of molasses, tomato paste, vinegar, and chipotle for a sticky, smoky finish that lingers like a good plot twist.

Real Talk Tip:
Keep a "coward's corner" on the grill. Not everyone wants to fight dragons at dinner. Have a milder version, labelled kindly, and nobody has to cry into their coleslaw.

Spicy Comfort Food with a Twist

After the outdoor theatrics of BBQ, with flaming ribs, oat milk disasters, and neighbours casually "dropping by", you'd think we'd settle down a bit, right? Nah. We're heading indoors. But not for peace and quiet. We're here for comfort food that kicks back. The kind that hugs you and headbutts you. You know, warm, cheesy, saucy classics that someone left alone in a room with a chilli and now have opinions.

Comfort food is emotional. It's nostalgic. It's the edible version of putting on fluffy socks and binge-watching your ex's new partner's Instagram stories. But here's the twist: when you introduce a bit of heat, that soft, safe dish suddenly gets... dangerous. In a good way.

Let me tell you what happened the night I brought chilli mac and cheese to a potluck. People assumed it was just your average creamy carb bomb. But I'd snuck in smoked chipotle, a hint of cayenne, and a spicy breadcrumb topping. The room went silent. Someone whispered, "Is this... spiritual?" One guy put down his fork and said, "I think I just forgave my father." I didn't ask questions. I just made a second tray.

That's the power of comfort food with edge. It's familiar, but fearless.

Here are a few legends with a little fire under the blanket:

FIERY MAC & CHEESE

THE CREAMY CARB BOMB THAT BITES BACK

YIELD: SERVES 6-8

HEAT LEVEL: 🌶🌶 (MEDIUM)

INGREDIENTS:

- 500g macaroni
- 4 tbsp butter
- 1/4 cup plain flour
- 4 cups milk
- 3 cups sharp cheddar, grated
- 1 cup Monterey Jack or Gouda, grated
- 2 tsp chipotle paste (or 1 tsp cayenne pepper)
- 1 tsp smoked paprika
- Salt and black pepper to taste
- For the topping: 1 cup panko breadcrumbs, 2 tbsp melted butter, 1 tsp sriracha

METHOD:

1. Cook the macaroni according to package directions until al dente. Drain and set aside.
2. Preheat your oven to 190°C (375°F).
3. In a large pot, melt the butter over medium heat. Whisk in the flour and cook for 1 minute to make a roux.
4. Gradually whisk in the milk until smooth. Cook, stirring constantly, until the sauce thickens, about 5-7 minutes.
5. Remove from heat and stir in the grated cheeses until melted and smooth. Stir in the chipotle paste and smoked paprika. Season with salt and pepper.
6. Fold the cooked macaroni into the cheese sauce until well coated. Pour into a large baking dish.
7. Mix the panko breadcrumbs with the melted butter and sriracha. Sprinkle evenly over the macaroni.
8. Bake for 20-25 minutes, until the topping is golden and the sauce is bubbly. Let it rest for 5 minutes before serving.

SPICY SHEPHERD'S PIE

A COMFORTING CLASSIC WITH A GARAM MASALA KICK.

YIELD: SERVES 6 **HEAT LEVEL: 🌶🌶 (MEDIUM)**

INGREDIENTS:

- 1 tbsp olive oil
- 1 large onion, chopped
- 2 carrots, diced
- 500g lamb or beef mince
- 2 cloves garlic, minced
- 1-2 fresh red chillies, finely chopped
- 2 tbsp hot sauce (e.g., Sriracha or Peri-Peri), mixed into the mashed potatoes
- 1 tbsp garam masala
- 1/2 tsp ground cinnamon
- 2 tbsp tomato paste
- 1 cup beef or vegetable stock
- 1 cup frozen peas
- 1.5 kg potatoes, peeled and quartered
- 1/2 cup milk
- 4 tbsp butter
- Salt and pepper to taste

METHOD:

1. Preheat oven to 200°C (400°F).
2. Boil the potatoes until tender. Drain, then mash with milk, butter, and the hot sauce. Season with salt and pepper. Set aside.
3. While potatoes are cooking, heat oil in a large ovenproof skillet over medium heat. Sauté onion and carrots until softened, about 5-7 minutes.
4. Add the mince and cook until browned. Add garlic, chilli, garam masala, and cinnamon; cook for 1 minute until fragrant.
5. Stir in tomato paste, then pour in the stock. Simmer for 10-15 minutes until the sauce has thickened. Stir in the frozen peas. Season to taste.
6. Spread the mashed potatoes evenly over the mince mixture. Use a fork to create peaks on top, which will brown nicely.
7. Bake for 20-25 minutes, or until the topping is golden and the filling is bubbling.

According to Shepherd (2006), the sensory interplay between spice and creamy fats like cheese enhances satisfaction by hitting multiple receptors at once. In other words, it tastes like therapy.
According to McGee (2004), spicy compounds like capsaicin actually change how our bodies perceive warmth, which makes hot dishes feel extra cozy. Tamang et al. (2016) explains how fermented chilli pastes in curries activate umami taste pathways, which increase satiety and flavour perception.

Chilli-Stewed Meats & Veggie Stars

Welcome to the simmering, bubbling, low-and-slow world of chilli-stewed legends. If BBQ was your loud-mouthed cousin who sings karaoke in public, and spicy comfort food was your friend who cries watching baking shows, then this section? This is the wise elder with secrets in a pot and a wooden spoon in hand. Calm. Deep. And absolutely unforgettable.

We're talking stews that change lives. The kind of dishes that make people stay for "just one more spoon." The kind that fills your home with a smell so rich, your neighbour starts checking if it's their birthday. And yes, we're putting chillies right in the middle of the cauldron, because in a stew, they don't punch. They haunt. Softly. Slowly. Deliciously.

Let's start with this: chilli in stews doesn't attack like it does in salsas or sauces. In liquid, with time, it mellows. It melts. It mingles. Think of it like a tough guy in a hot bath, still intense, but now philosophical.

Here's how to make chilli-stewed dishes sing:

1. Choose Your Chillies Wisely
For meat-based stews, go bold: use ancho, chipotle, guajillo, or scotch bonnet (if you're prepared to explain the dish before serving). These bring deep, earthy flavour with varying degrees of heat. According to Bosland and Votava (2012), dried chillies develop complex, wine-like undertones when rehydrated, making them ideal for long cooks.
For vegetarian stews? Lean into smoked paprika, Aleppo pepper, or fresh jalapeños. You want the veg to shine, not hide under a fire blanket. Stews with sweet potatoes, lentils, or black beans love a gentle heat that builds.

2. Build From the Base
Start with onions, garlic, and chillies, sautéed in oil until soft and fragrant. Add your spices. Then layer your proteins and vegetables. Add stock, crushed tomatoes, coconut milk, whatever liquid your stew calls for. Let it go low and slow. The capsaicin breaks down beautifully over time, blending with fat and acid to create smooth, rich warmth (Shepherd, 2006).

3. Don't Forget the Finishers
A splash of lime. A swirl of yoghurt. A fistful of fresh herbs. These bright flavours contrast the long-cooked depth and keep things from feeling heavy.

According to McGee (2004), acidity helps lift and balance dishes, especially where spice is involved.

MEXICAN-INSPIRED BEEF & ANCHO STEW

SLOW-COOKED, RICH, AND DEEPLY SATISFYING WITH A SMOKY WARMTH

YIELD: SERVES 6

HEAT LEVEL: 🌶🌶 (MEDIUM)

INGREDIENTS:

- 3 dried ancho chillies
- 2 tbsp olive oil
- 1.5 kg beef chuck, cut into 3cm cubes
- 1 large onion, chopped
- 4 cloves garlic, minced
- 1 tsp ground cumin
- 1 tsp dried oregano
- 1 tbsp cocoa powder
- 400g can crushed tomatoes
- 4 cups beef stock
- Salt and pepper to taste
- To serve: warm tortillas, sour cream, coriander

METHOD:

1. Remove stems and seeds from the ancho chillies. Tear into pieces and cover with boiling water. Let soak for 20 minutes until soft. Blend into a smooth paste.

2. Pat the beef dry and season generously with salt and pepper. Heat oil in a large, heavy-based pot over medium-high heat and brown the beef in batches. Set aside.

3. In the same pot, sauté the onion until soft, about 5 minutes. Add the garlic, cumin, and oregano; cook for 1 minute until fragrant.

4. Return the beef to the pot. Stir in the ancho chilli paste, cocoa powder, crushed tomatoes, and beef stock. Bring to a boil.

5. Reduce heat to low, cover, and simmer gently for 2.5 - 3 hours, until the beef is fork-tender.

6. Season to taste. Serve with warm tortillas, a dollop of sour cream, and fresh coriander.

WEST AFRICAN PEANUT & SCOTCH BONNET STEW

CREAMY, RICH, AND FIERCELY FLAVOURFUL.

YIELD: SERVES 6

HEAT LEVEL: 🌶🌶🌶 (HOT)

INGREDIENTS:

- 2 tbsp red palm oil or vegetable oil
- 1 large onion, chopped
- 3 cloves garlic, minced
- 1 tbsp fresh ginger, grated
- 1-2 Scotch bonnet chillies, pierced with a knife (do not chop)
- 500g chicken thighs, skinless and boneless (or 1 large sweet potato, peeled and cubed for a veggie version)
- 1 red bell pepper, chopped
- 400g can crushed tomatoes
- 4 cups chicken or vegetable stock
- 1 cup smooth, natural peanut butter
- Salt and pepper to taste
- To serve: cooked rice or fufu, chopped spring onions

METHOD:

1. Heat the oil in a large pot over medium heat. Sauté the onion until softened, about 5 minutes. Add the garlic and ginger; cook for 1 minute.

2. Add the chicken (or sweet potato) and brown lightly. Add the whole Scotch bonnet chillies and red bell pepper; stir to combine.

3. Pour in the crushed tomatoes and stock. Bring to a boil, then reduce heat and simmer for 30 minutes (or until sweet potato is tender).

4. Remove the Scotch bonnet chillies (they can be left in for more heat, but warn your guests!).

5. In a bowl, thin the peanut butter with a ladleful of the hot stew liquid, then stir this mixture back into the pot.

6. Simmer for another 15-20 minutes until the stew has thickened. Season with salt and pepper. Serve over rice or with fufu, garnished with spring onions.

Making Mains with Global Flare

If you've stuck with me this far, congratulations, you're no longer just a chilli enthusiast. You are a globe-trotting flavour bandit with spice-stained fingers and a very smug grin.

We've tackled barbecues that singe eyebrows. We've tucked into comfort food with emotional baggage. We've ladled out stews that could double as therapy. But now, we're packing our passports (and our spice jars) to cook mains that scream bold, spicy, global joy. This isn't fusion-for-the-sake-of-it nonsense. This is intentional chaos. The good kind. The "oh-my-god-what-is-in-this?" kind.

Let's be honest. Food is the original passport. And chillies? They're the ink. From Korea to Jamaica, Thailand to Morocco, chillies connect people like gossip and Wi-Fi. So if you're ready to level up your mains, let's take that chilli and let it travel.

Global Mains That Bring the Heat and the Hype:

JAMAICAN JERK CHICKEN

FIERCELY FRAGRANT AND UNAPOLOGETICALLY FIERY.

YIELD: SERVES 4-6 **HEAT LEVEL: 🌶🌶🌶 (HOT)**

INGREDIENTS:

- 1.5 kg chicken pieces (thighs and drumsticks work best)
- 6 spring onions, chopped
- 4 cloves garlic
- 2-3 Scotch bonnet chillies, stems removed
- 2 tbsp fresh thyme leaves
- 1 tbsp allspice berries (or 2 tsp ground allspice)
- 1 tsp ground cinnamon
- 1 tsp ground nutmeg
- 1/2 cup soy sauce
- 2 tbsp vegetable oil
- Juice of 2 limes
- 1 tbsp brown sugar

METHOD:

1. Place all ingredients except the chicken into a blender or food processor. Blend until a coarse paste forms.

2. Make deep slashes in the chicken pieces and place them in a large bowl or zip-top bag. Pour the marinade over the chicken, ensuring it gets into the slashes. Marinate for at least 4 hours, preferably overnight.

3. Preheat your grill to medium-high heat. Grill the chicken for 25-35 minutes, turning occasionally, until cooked through and slightly charred. Alternatively, bake in a 200°C (400°F) oven for 30-40 minutes.

KOREAN SPICY PORK BULGOGI (DWAEJI BULGOGI)

SWEET, SALTY, SPICY, AND INCREDIBLY MOREISH.

YIELD: SERVES 4

HEAT LEVEL: 🌶🌶 (MEDIUM)

INGREDIENTS:

- 500g pork shoulder or belly, thinly sliced
- 1/2 Asian pear, grated (or 1 tbsp brown sugar)
- 4 cloves garlic, minced
- 1 tbsp fresh ginger, grated
- 4 tbsp gochujang (Korean chilli paste)
- To serve: lettuce leaves, steamed rice, kimchi
- 2 tbsp soy sauce
- 1 tbsp sesame oil
- 2 tsp gochugaru (Korean chilli flakes)
- 1 tbsp honey or maple syrup
- 2 spring onions, sliced
- 1 tbsp toasted sesame seeds

METHOD:

1. In a bowl, combine the grated pear, garlic, ginger, gochujang, soy sauce, sesame oil, gochugaru, and honey. Mix well.

2. Add the sliced pork to the marinade, ensuring each piece is coated. Let it marinate for at least 30 minutes.

3. Heat a large skillet or wok over high heat. Add the marinated pork and cook, stirring frequently, for 5-7 minutes until cooked through and caramelised.

4. Stir in the spring onions and sesame seeds. Serve immediately with lettuce leaves for wrapping and steamed rice.

THAI BASIL CHILLI CHICKEN (PAD KRAPOW GAI)

A LIGHTNING-FAST STIR-FRY THAT PACKS AN AROMATIC PUNCH.

YIELD: SERVES 2-3 **HEAT LEVEL:))) (HOT)**

INGREDIENTS:

- 2 tbsp vegetable oil
- 4 cloves garlic, minced
- 2-4 Thai bird's eye chillies, finely chopped (adjust to taste)
- 500g chicken mince
- 2 tbsp oyster sauce
- 1 tbsp soy sauce
- 1 tsp fish sauce
- 1 tsp dark soy sauce (for colour, optional)
- 1 tsp sugar
- 1 large handful of holy basil or Thai basil leaves
- To serve: jasmine rice, fried eggs

METHOD:

1. Heat the oil in a wok or large skillet over high heat. Add the garlic and chillies and stir-fry for 30 seconds until fragrant.
2. Add the chicken mince and break it up with a spatula. Cook until no longer pink.
3. Add the oyster sauce, soy sauce, fish sauce, dark soy sauce, and sugar. Stir-fry for another 2-3 minutes until the sauce coats the chicken.
4. Turn off the heat and stir in the basil leaves until just wilted.
5. Serve immediately over jasmine rice, topped with a crispy fried egg.

Quick Tips for Global Flare without Kitchen Meltdown:

- Keep lemons, yoghurt, and fresh herbs handy. They cool things down and make your plate look intentional.
- Use one hero spice paste or chilli per dish. No need to mix Peri-Peri with gochujang and jerk rub unless your goal is divorce by dinner.
- Learn a dish's origin story. It's fun, it's respectful, and you'll sound like a spicy genius when people ask, "What is this?"

7 SPICE FOR THE MILD-MANNERED

Before we charge into flavour with flamethrowers again, let's pause, breathe, and honour the quietly brave: the spice-curious but chilli-cautious. Yes, I see you, reaching for the mild salsa at parties, quietly asking if the curry is "on the gentle side," sipping water after that one rogue jalapeño incident in 2014. This chapter? It's yours.

Because not everyone wants to sweat through their socks or chant through chilli tears. And that's okay. Spice doesn't have to be a dare. It can be a whisper. A hint. A soft glow instead of a house fire. And frankly, some of the best dishes use heat like perfume—not poured, but delicately dabbed behind the ears.

We've just globetrotted through some pretty fiery mains, but now we're pulling back the heat dial and leaning into balance. Into grace. Into flavour-first, fuss-second food that still sings without screaming.

So, whether you're cooking for spice-sensitive friends, kids, or just easing yourself into the wide, wonderful world of chilli, this chapter's full of warmth, not war.

Because trust me, you don't need five-alarm flames to make a dish worth remembering.

Gentle Heat for Shy Palates

Let's get something straight: gentle heat is not boring. It's not bland. And it's definitely not some sad compromise between "fun" and "digestively safe." Gentle heat is a quiet confidence. It's the Chillies Whisperer. The type of spice that leans in instead of shouting across the room.

Think of it like good jazz. It doesn't need to break windows to move you. It just needs timing, depth, and the ability to surprise you with a little flourish when you least expect it.

So if you've got that one friend who claims black pepper is "a bit much," or maybe you are the person who sniffs at the idea of a Vindaloo, congratulations. This section is your VIP lounge.

Here's how I approach gentle heat in a way that brings flavour without triggering fire alarms or family trauma.

1. Use Sweet Chillies as Your Base

Chillies like poblano, banana peppers, or mild cherry peppers bring body and flavour without burning the tongue. Poblano in particular has a smoky, earthy note that makes stews, roasts, and sauces feel indulgent without feeling dangerous. According to Bosland and Votava (2012), these varieties clock in under 2,000 Scoville Heat Units, which is like the chilli version of a polite handshake.
Try roasting poblanos, then blending them into a creamy sauce with garlic, lime, and yoghurt. Serve over grilled veg or chicken. Instant depth. Zero drama.

2. Add Chilli Oil by the Drop, Not the Drench

Instead of cooking with chilli, finish the dish with a controlled drizzle. Chilli oil, especially if you've made it yourself with milder flakes like Aleppo pepper, gives that "ooh" moment without the "oh no." Aleppo, by the way, is slightly tangy, warm, and often compared to sun-dried tomato vibes with an attitude (McGee, 2004).
Drizzle it on roasted butternut squash, swirl it into hummus, or dot it onto scrambled eggs. It's like accessorizing with hot sauce earrings instead of a flamethrower necklace.

3. Use Dairy to Carry the Heat

Let's take a moment to thank cheese, cream, and yoghurt for being chilli's best babysitter. These cooling agents bond with capsaicin and mellow out the fire while letting flavour bloom. Shepherd (2006) explains that dairy fats reduce the burn by physically dissolving capsaicin oils, making the sensation smoother and less aggressive.
Think spicy yoghurt dressings, cream cheese dips with jalapeño jelly, or goat cheese whipped with smoked paprika and just a tickle of cayenne.

4. Use Citrus and Fresh Herbs as Chilli's Support Team

Acidic flavours like lime, lemon, and vinegar sharpen taste buds and balance heat beautifully. Combine that with herbs like mint, coriander, or parsley and

you've got dishes that tingle, not tangle.
One of my go-to's? A couscous salad with roasted red pepper, chopped parsley, preserved lemon, and a dash of chilli oil. It whispers heat but winks with flavour.

Real-life moment?
I once brought a sweet potato gratin to a potluck. I infused the cream with garlic and just a pinch of Aleppo pepper, topped it with parmesan, and baked it until golden. A man in his sixties took a bite and said, "This tastes like my childhood, but better." He had no idea there was chilli in it. Just warmth. That's the sweet spot.

Tips for Serving Mixed-Spice Crowds

Alright, brave cook. Let's talk about the spice spectrum, that glorious, chaotic buffet of human tolerance ranging from "Is there even pepper in this?" to "Do you have a fire extinguisher for my tongue?"

You know the type. Aunt Carol starts sweating if her tea's too gingery. Meanwhile, your cousin brings his own ghost pepper flakes in a keychain grinder and mutters, "This is baby food" under his breath at the buffet. Cooking for both? That's not just a meal; it's a diplomatic mission.

So how do you throw a chilli-friendly feast that doesn't end in tears, lawsuits, or someone dramatically spooning yoghurt into their mouth like it's a medical emergency?

Let's get into it. Grab your apron. Channel your inner peacekeeper. Because feeding mixed-spice guests is a culinary high-wire act, and you're about to cross it in style.

1. Build a "Choose Your Own Heat" Table
Don't gamble with people's tongues. Set up a spread with base dishes that are flavourful but mild. Then offer spice on the side like a condiment station from a hot sauce heaven. Think of it like chilli toppings with personality:

- **Mild:** Jalapeño jam, smoky paprika oil
- **Medium:** Chipotle crema, sriracha yoghurt, chilli chutney
- **Wild:** Scotch bonnet sauce in a glass vial with a label that says "Use at Your Own Risk (And Don't Sue Me)"

This way, no one gets ambushed, and everyone feels seen.
According to McGee (2004), capsaicin doesn't cook out the way salt or sugar does; it clings. So the moment you stir heat into the whole dish, you've made a choice on behalf of every mouth at the table. Make it optional instead. Be generous and strategic.

2. Use the "Two-Tier Trick"

If you're making something like chilli mac, stew, or curry, split the batch. One pot gets the fiery treatment. The other stays warm, mild, and friendly. This doesn't double your effort. It halves your regrets.
I once made a Thai green curry for a mixed crowd and labelled the pots "Polite" and "Possessed." A guy named Liam mixed both together and said, "This is how I reclaim my childhood." Whatever that means, he went back for thirds.

3. Make Cooling Sides That Actually Taste Good

Don't just serve yoghurt. Make it sing. Try:

- Mint & cucumber raita
- Lime-avocado crema
- Feta whipped with lemon and parsley

These not only tame the heat; they elevate the dish. Shepherd (2006) explains that when cooling ingredients hit the same taste pathways as heat (like fat, acid, or texture), they don't mute; they balance.
Bonus: they also make you look like the kind of host who knows their stuff and cares about people's tongues. Win-win.

4. Label Like a Legend

Create cards. Colour code. Draw fire emojis if you must. I once saw a party where dips were rated with chilli icons, from 1 (barely awake) to 5 (call your therapist). Not only was it helpful, it became the thing guests talked about. And if you're feeling cheeky, write "Safe Zone" or "No Shame Corner" next to the mild ones. Trust me, even spice warriors sneak back there after a round with the ghost pepper wings.

Cooling Sides, Dips, and Drinks

Okay. So, your guests have tangoed with a chipotle burger. Wrestled a jalapeño popper. Perhaps had a minor identity crisis mid-curry. And now, they're fanning their mouths, breathing like they've just run a 5K through a volcano.

Time to play the hero.

Because for every spicy dish that sets taste buds ablaze, there needs to be a cooling companion waiting with a metaphorical hug, a cold compress, and maybe a side of mint. Welcome to the unsung heroes of the spicy table: dips, sides, and drinks that save lives. Or at least stop your uncle from crying into the guacamole.

Last section, we tackled the chaos of feeding a mixed-spice crowd. This time, we're building a chilli emergency kit disguised as deliciousness. Think of it like emotional support food for heat survivors.

1. Creamy Dips That Don't Taste Like Boring Apologies

First rule: don't let cooling dips be bland. You're not applying wallpaper paste. You're creating edible relief with flavour.

AVOCADO-LIME YOGHURT DIP

CREAMY, ZESTY, AND HEROIC.

YIELD: SERVES 6-8 **HEAT LEVEL: (COOLING)**

INGREDIENTS:

- 1 ripe avocado
- 1 cup Greek yoghurt
- Juice of 1 lime
- 2 tbsp fresh coriander, chopped
- 1/4 tsp ground cumin
- Salt to taste

METHOD:

1. Scoop the avocado flesh into a bowl and mash with a fork until smooth.
2. Add the Greek yoghurt, lime juice, coriander, and cumin. Mix until well combined.
3. Season with salt to taste. Serve immediately with veggie sticks or crackers.

Fats in dairy and avocado physically dissolve capsaicin, the compound that makes chilli feel like betrayal in the mouth (Shepherd, 2006). That's why these dips don't just cool; they neutralise.

I once brought my avocado-lime yoghurt dip to a spicy wings night. The guy who mocked "mild options" early on? He later tried to steal the bowl and whispered, "I can taste colour again."

2. Cooling Sides That Feel Like a Reset Button

Balance the heat bomb with sides that refresh. Your goal is texture, temperature, and contrast.

CUCUMBER & POMEGRANATE SALAD

CRUNCHY, SWEET, AND REFRESHINGLY COOL.

YIELD: SERVES 4 **HEAT LEVEL:) (WARM)**

INGREDIENTS:

- 2 large cucumbers, finely diced
- 1/2 cup pomegranate seeds
- 1/4 red onion, very thinly sliced
- 2 tbsp fresh mint, chopped
- Zest and juice of 1 lemon
- 1 tbsp olive oil
- Salt and pepper to taste

METHOD:

1. In a large bowl, combine the diced cucumber, pomegranate seeds, red onion, and mint.

2. In a small jar, shake together the lemon zest, lemon juice, and olive oil to make a dressing.

3. Pour the dressing over the salad and toss gently. Season with salt and pepper. Serve chilled.

According to McGee (2004), high water content foods like cucumber and watermelon soothe not just the palate, but the whole eating experience. Add something crunchy, something salty, and suddenly your meal goes from "mouth battle" to "balanced harmony."
True story: I once served a mango and mint salad alongside fiery Peruvian chicken. The salad was gone before the meat. When asked if it was dessert, I said, "It's first aid."

3. Drinks That Actually Help (No, Not Water)

Repeat after me: Water spreads capsaicin. Milk dissolves it. Citrus distracts it. Alcohol… complicates it.

SOOTHING MANGO LASSI

SWEET, COLD, AND THICKER THAN YOUR EX'S EXCUSES.

YIELD: SERVES 2 **HEAT LEVEL: 🌶 (WARM)**

INGREDIENTS:

- 1 cup ripe mango, chopped (fresh or frozen)
- 1 cup plain yoghurt
- 1/2 cup milk
- 1 tbsp honey or sugar (optional, to taste)
- A pinch of cardamom (optional)
- Ice cubes

METHOD:

1. Combine all ingredients in a blender.
2. Blend until smooth and frothy.
3. Pour into glasses and serve immediately.

Prescott and Stevenson (1996) found that drinks with sweetness and viscosity (thickness) coat the mouth, blunting the burn more effectively than plain liquids. So yes, serve the mango lassi. And serve it proud.

Pro tip: make a "chilli cooldown station" at your party. Stack it with yoghurt dips, fresh-cut fruit, and icy jugs of calming drinks. Label it "Refuge Area." Everyone will laugh. Then silently head there after that third spoon of scotch bonnet stew.

Mild Doesn't Mean Boring

Let's kill a myth today, shall we? A big, bloated, overused myth that's long overdue for a proper funeral: that mild food = boring food. Lies. Slander. Absolute nonsense. Saying mild food is boring is like saying a string quartet is less talented than a rock band because it's not loud.

No. Flavour isn't volume. It's balance. It's intention. It's the difference between shouting and being heard. And mild food, when done right, sings.

We've just pampered our guests with soothing dips and chill-out drinks after their fiery feasts. Now let's talk about mild dishes that steal the show without setting your eyebrows on fire. Because here's the secret: when you take the heat out, you make room for depth.

1. Mild Doesn't Mean Flavourless; It Means Focused

When there's no big chilli punch, your tongue has time to notice all the background dancers: the citrus, the herbs, the warm spices. Cinnamon. Cumin. Coriander. These aren't just "filler" flavours. These are the smooth operators.

Take something like a turmeric and coconut dal. No heat. Just golden, earthy comfort with a whisper of ginger and lemon. It tastes like a spa day in a bowl. According to McGee (2004), spices like turmeric and ginger trigger subtle sensory responses, especially when combined with fats that help release their essential oils. That's why a simple mild curry can taste so layered it feels… personal.

2. Texture Is Your Best Friend

If you're not smacking people in the face with spice, give their mouths something to do.

Think:

- Crunchy toasted nuts on top of soft stews
- Creamy hummus with crisp veg and chewy flatbread
- Roasted root veg with crispy edges and soft centres

Mouthfeel matters. Shepherd (2006) found that our brains interpret texture alongside flavour, which is why crunchy food tastes more exciting, even if it's not spicy. So play with contrast. Add toasted seeds, pomegranate pops, or even a slick of good olive oil. Boom, now your mild dish has swagger.

3. Acidity + Freshness = Instant Lift

A squeeze of lemon. A drizzle of vinegar. A spoon of yoghurt. These bright elements wake up a dish like a fan in a hot room. They don't make food spicy, but they make it sparkle. You're not adding fire; you're turning up the lights. For example, I once made a lentil salad with parsley, lemon zest, olive oil, and roasted sweet potato. It had no heat at all, yet one guest asked, "Is this spicy?" Nope. Just punchy. That's the magic of acidity and aromatics working in harmony.

4. Don't Be Afraid of Sweet + Savoury

Mild food gives you room to play. So go wild with combos:

- Feta + watermelon + mint
- Roasted carrot + harissa honey glaze (just a whisper!)
- Apple slices with sharp cheddar

Prescott and Stevenson (1996) observed that novelty in taste pairings (like sweet and salty) increases perceived enjoyment, even when spice levels are low. Mild food lets these pairings shine.

Real Talk: Mild Food Doesn't Apologise

It doesn't need to. Because when you balance herbs, acidity, sweetness, creaminess, and crunch, who needs heat? If your dish makes someone pause, smile, and go in for seconds, it's already won. Fire or no fire.

8 FIRE MEETS SWEET: SPICY DESSERTS

"All you need is love. But a little chocolate now and then doesn't hurt." – Charles M. Schulz

Charles, bless him, clearly never had chilli-spiked chocolate truffles. Because if he had, he might've added: *"...especially if it sets your soul and your tastebuds on fire in one silky bite."*

Welcome to the chapter where sugar meets sass. Where desserts don't just sweeten the deal; they set the rules. And you? You've made it here like the chilli gladiator you are. From gentle palates and diplomatic dinners to bold barbecues and cooling yoghurt rescues, you've simmered, stirred, and survived.

Now it's time to flip the table. Because who said spice should clock out at dessert? Absolutely not. In this chapter, chilli becomes your pastry sous-chef. It slips into chocolate. It whispers through fruit sorbets. It flirts with caramel like a guilty pleasure. And just when your guests think the heat parade is over, you serve up a dessert that makes them rethink everything they knew about sweets.

From chilli-dusted popcorn to exotic bakes with hidden heat, we're going full sugar-and-spice mode. No compromises. No apologies. Just wildly good endings with a warm twist.

Chilli Chocolate, the Ultimate Affair

You know those relationships your friends warn you about? The ones that start sweet, get intense, and leave you dramatically whispering, "I know it's wrong, but I can't stop"? That's chilli and chocolate. The most seductive food affair since butter met toast.

Seriously, if chilli chocolate had a Tinder profile, it'd be the one that says "likes long walks in the dark, passionate surprises, and melting on tongues." And you'd swipe right. Hard.

Now, before you clutch your pearls and scream "not my brownie!", let me tell you this: chilli doesn't ruin chocolate; it reveals it. It unlocks depth, balances sweetness, and adds just enough danger to make your dessert feel less "cupcake" and more "mysterious stranger with a secret." And don't just take my word for it. According to McGee (2004), capsaicin (the compound that brings the burn) activates the same sensory pathways as temperature and pleasure, which is why a small dose with rich fats (like cocoa butter) creates a whole-body *mmm* effect. Literal flavour flirtation.

The Science of Why It Works

Chocolate is loaded with fats and aromatics. It melts near body temperature, coating your mouth like a velvet hug. Chillies, especially when used in moderation, don't fight that texture. They tease it. Capsaicin hits the tongue just enough to add warmth, which wakes up your palate and makes the chocolate taste darker, richer, deeper. It's like switching your playlist from elevator music to Miles Davis.

Shepherd (2006) explains that smell and taste work together to shape flavour perception. So, when your nose picks up the cocoa, vanilla, and even the faint smokiness of dried chillies, your brain throws a party before the spoon even hits your mouth.

CHILLI CHOCOLATE TRUFFLES

DECADENT, DARK, AND WITH A MISCHIEVOUS KICK.

YIELD: MAKES 20-24 TRUFFLES **HEAT LEVEL: 🌶 (WARM)**

INGREDIENTS:

- 200g dark chocolate (70% cocoa), finely chopped
- 1/2 cup double cream
- 1/4 tsp cayenne pepper (or 1/2 tsp ancho chilli powder for a smokier note)
- 1/4 tsp ground cinnamon
- 2 tbsp unsalted butter, softened
- Cocoa powder, for dusting

METHOD:

1. Place the chopped chocolate in a heatproof bowl.
2. In a small saucepan, heat the cream, cayenne, and cinnamon over medium heat until it just begins to simmer.
3. Pour the hot cream over the chocolate. Let it sit for one minute, then stir gently from the centre outwards until the chocolate is completely melted and the mixture is smooth.
4. Stir in the softened butter until fully incorporated.
5. Cover the bowl and refrigerate for at least 3-4 hours, or until the ganache is firm enough to scoop.
6. Using a teaspoon or a melon baller, scoop out portions of the ganache and quickly roll them into balls between your palms. Place on a baking sheet lined with parchment paper.
7. Roll the truffles in cocoa powder to coat. Store in the refrigerator until ready to serve.

SPICED HOT CHOCOLATE WITH ATTITUDE

THE CLASSIC WINTER WARMER, NOW WITH A FIERY SOUL.

YIELD: SERVES 2

HEAT LEVEL: 🌶 (WARM)

INGREDIENTS:

- 2 cups milk (or oat milk for a dairy -free version)
- 100g dark chocolate, chopped
- 1 tbsp cocoa powder
- 1 tbsp brown sugar or maple syrup
- 1/4 tsp ground cinnamon
- A tiny pinch of cayenne pepper (or chilli powder)
- Whipped cream and extra chilli powder for garnish (optional)

METHOD:

1. In a small saucepan, whisk together the milk, chopped chocolate, cocoa powder, sugar, cinnamon, and cayenne.
2. Heat over medium-low heat, whisking constantly, until the chocolate is fully melted and the drink is hot and frothy. Do not boil
3. Taste and adjust sweetness or spice if needed.
4. Pour into mugs, top with whipped cream, and dust with a whisper of chilli powder for drama.

Prescott and Stevenson (1996) found that novel combinations in food, especially those that combine contrasting flavours and textures, increase perceived enjoyment. So yes, when you shock someone's mouth with spice and then soothe it with silky chocolate, their brain sends up a little firework.

Tips for Not Overdoing It

- Start small. You want the chilli to arrive fashionably late, not crash the party.
- Choose milder chillies like ancho, Aleppo, or guajillo if you're spice-shy.
- Remember: chilli gets stronger as it sits in chocolate. Taste after it cools, not just while it's warm and friendly.

Spiced Fruit Sorbets & Exotic Bakes

If chilli chocolate is the sultry midnight affair you text but never bring home to mum, then this section is its sun-kissed cousin—playful, exotic, a little cheeky, and dangerously good at brunch.

We're stepping into the world of fruity desserts with unexpected sass. Sorbets that cool you down while slapping your taste buds just a little. Cakes that look innocent until you realise they've got depth, mystery, and possibly a secret passport. These aren't your nan's apple pies. These are tropical fruit bombs with spicy aftershocks.

Last section, we dipped into chocolate's dark side and melted into truffles with secrets. But now? We're turning to bright flavours, the mangoes, pineapples, berries, and citrus fruits that already sing on their own, and giving them a chilli-flecked microphone. You in?

The Science of Spicy-Sweet Sorcery

Fruit brings natural sugars and acids, both of which play incredibly well with chilli. Capsaicin, that tongue-tingling firecracker, gets amplified by sugar but balanced by acid, which is why mango with chilli tastes like a carnival while mango alone just feels... polite.

According to Shepherd (2006), acidic ingredients enhance volatile aromatics, which means adding a squeeze of lime or a dash of vinegar to chilli-laced desserts literally makes them smell better and taste sharper. It's food flirting with your brain.

MANGO-LIME-CHILLI SORBET

BRIGHT, BOLD, AND REFRESHING WITH A WARM FINISH.

YIELD: SERVES 4-6 **HEAT LEVEL: 🌶 (WARM)**

INGREDIENTS:

- 3 cups ripe mango, chopped (fresh or frozen)
- 1/2 cup sugar (or to taste)
- 1/2 cup water
- Juice of 2 limes
- Zest of 1 lime
- A pinch of salt
- 1/4 tsp cayenne pepper (or Aleppo pepper flakes)

METHOD:

1. In a small saucepan, combine the sugar and water. Heat over medium, stirring until the sugar dissolves completely. This is your simple syrup. Let it cool.
2. In a blender, combine the mango, cooled simple syrup, lime juice, lime zest, salt, and cayenne. Blend until completely smooth.
3. Churn the mixture in an ice cream maker according to the manufacturer's instructions.
4. Transfer to a lidded container and freeze for at least 4 hours, or until firm.
5. No ice cream maker? Pour the blended mixture into a shallow dish and freeze. After 2 hours, scrape and stir with a fork to break up ice crystals. Repeat every 30-45 minutes until you achieve a fluffy, sorbet-like texture.

ORANGE & CARDAMOM CAKE WITH CHILLI GLAZE

A FRAGRANT, MOIST CAKE WITH A ZESTY, SPICY GLAZE.

YIELD: SERVES 8-10

HEAT LEVEL: 🌶 (WARM)

INGREDIENTS:

- For the cake:
  - 2 large oranges
  - 200g ground almonds
  - 150g caster sugar
  - 3 large eggs
  - 1 tsp baking powder
  - 1 tsp ground cardamom
- For the glaze:
  - 1 cup icing sugar
  - 2-3 tbsp orange juice
  - 1/2 tsp chilli flakes, lightly crushed

METHOD:

1. Preheat oven to 180°C (160°C Fan). Grease and line a 20cm round cake tin.
2. Boil the whole oranges in water for 1 hour until very soft. Drain, let cool, then cut open and remove any seeds. Pulp the entire oranges (skin and all) in a food processor.
3. In a large bowl, mix the orange pulp, ground almonds, sugar, eggs, baking powder, and cardamom until well combined
4. Pour the batter into the prepared tin and bake for 45-55 minutes, or until a skew inserted into the centre comes out clean. Let the cake cool completely in the tin.
5. For the glaze, whisk the icing sugar with enough orange juice to make a thick but pourable consistency. Stir in the crushed chilli flakes.
6. Pour the glaze over the cooled cake, allowing it to drizzle down the sides.

Both recipes hit sweet, sour, and spicy—what McGee (2004) calls the trifecta of flavour layering, essential for memorable dishes.
Prescott and Stevenson (1996) found that novelty in food (like chilli in desserts) increases engagement and enjoyment. So yes, when you serve a cake that tastes like a tropical vacation with a kick, your guests will remember you forever.

A Note on Balance

- Chillies in cold desserts feel brighter. Keep your dose small.
- Citrus and ginger can mimic heat, so use them to stretch flavour without going full flamethrower.
- Always taste after chilling; cold dulls spice, so what feels subtle warm may vanish once frozen.

Chilli-Caramel Popcorn & Snackables

Some desserts wear pearls and call you "darling." Others show up in ripped jeans, steal your fries, and set your mouth on fire, and that's exactly where we are now. Welcome to the messy, crunchy, dangerously snackable world of chilli-caramel popcorn, nuts, brittle, and other mischief-makers of the dessert table.

You've swirled your way through chilli chocolate seduction, flirted with frozen sorbets, and danced with citrus-laced exotic bakes. But now? Now we snack. Now we scatter spice across the living room floor like confetti. These aren't fancy plated finales. These are the grab-a-handful-and-regret-nothing champions. The "I'll just try one" villains that become "...okay, who ate the whole bowl?"

And chilli? Oh, it fits in beautifully. Because sweet, sticky, salty, crunchy—that's the holy quartet of addiction. And adding just a tickle of heat to the mix doesn't just make sense; it makes magic.

Let's Talk Texture

Caramel popcorn is already the bad boy of the snack world. Add chilli, and it becomes a rockstar with a flamethrower guitar. That crunch? It's essential. Texture not only creates satisfaction; it heightens flavour perception, according to Shepherd (2006). That first bite? It explodes. That slow burn at the end? It lingers.
McGee (2004) explains that sugar, when cooked to caramel stage, enhances the aromatic compounds of other ingredients. Which means chilli doesn't just sit there awkwardly; it blooms. Like a firecracker wrapped in a hug.

CHILLI-CARAMEL POPCORN

THE ULTIMATE SWEET, SALTY, AND SPICY SNACK.

YIELD: SERVES 6-8 AS A SNACK **HEAT LEVEL: 🌶🌶 (MEDIUM)**

INGREDIENTS:

- 10 cups plain popped popcorn (about 1/2 cup unpopped kernels)
- 1 cup brown sugar
- 1/2 cup unsalted butter
- 1/4 cup golden syrup or light corn syrup
- 1/2 tsp baking soda
- 1 tsp vanilla extract
- 1 tsp flaky sea salt
- 1/2 - 1 tsp cayenne pepper (adjust to taste)

METHOD:

1. Preheat oven to 120°C (100°C Fan). Line a large baking tray with parchment paper and spread the popped popcorn on it, removing any unpopped kernels.

2. In a medium saucepan over medium heat, melt the butter. Stir in the brown sugar and golden syrup. Bring to a boil and let it bubble for 4-5 minutes without stirring.

3. Remove from heat and immediately stir in the baking soda, vanilla, sea salt, and cayenne pepper. The mixture will foam up.

4. Quickly pour the hot caramel over the popcorn and use two spatulas to toss and coat everything evenly.

5. Bake for 1 hour, stirring every 20 minutes.

6. Let the popcorn cool completely on the tray before breaking it into chunks. Store in an airtight container.

SPICED NUT CLUSTERS

CRUNCHY, ADDICTIVE, AND PERFECT FOR GIFTING (IF THEY LAST).

YIELD: MAKES ABOUT 2 CUPS OF CLUSTERS

HEAT LEVEL: (MEDIUM)

INGREDIENTS:

- 2 cups mixed raw nuts (e.g., almonds, pecans, cashews)
- 3 tbsp honey
- 1 tbsp brown sugar
- 1 tbsp butter
- 1/2 tsp smoked paprika
- 1/4 tsp cayenne pepper
- 1/2 tsp flaky sea salt

METHOD:

1. Preheat oven to 180°C (160°C Fan). Line a baking sheet with parchment paper.
2. In a bowl, toss the nuts with the honey, brown sugar, butter, smoked paprika, and cayenne until evenly coated.
3. Spread the mixture in a single layer on the prepared baking sheet.
4. Bake for 10-12 minutes, stirring halfway, until the nuts are golden and fragrant.
5. Sprinkle with flaky sea salt while still warm. Let them cool completely—they will clump into delicious clusters as they cool.

Prescott and Stevenson (1996) found that sweet and spicy combinations, when texturally satisfying, stimulate both reward and novelty centres in the brain. Translation: you'll want more, even when you shouldn't.

Tips for Snack Success

- Keep your chilli measured. A whisper, not a war.
- Use smoked, fruity, or mild chillies like Aleppo, chipotle, or even urfa for layers instead of shock.
- Always cool completely before storing, unless you want soggy regret in a Tupperware.

Real-Life Confession

I once made a batch of chilli-caramel popcorn "for the party." I tasted it "just to check." An hour later, I was at the supermarket buying more corn. I told guests it got "lost in transport." I lied. I don't regret it.

Sweet Heat Pairings to Impress

Let's be honest, some dishes make people say "Yum." Others make them close their eyes, whisper your name like it's sacred, and text their therapist to unpack the feelings. Welcome to that second category.

This final dessert section isn't just about ending a meal; it's about ending it with swagger. This is where you stop playing it safe and start pairing sweet with heat like a flavour mixologist on a mission. Because if chilli has taught us anything, it's that it doesn't just belong in mains. Or sauces. Or popcorn. It belongs wherever drama, delight, and a little "oooh" are welcome.

So far in this chapter, we've courted chocolate, seduced sorbets, and turned snack time into a crunchy fever dream. Now, we wrap things up with fancy-but-doable pairings you can whip out at dinner parties, romantic nights in, or Tuesday afternoons when you just need a win.

The Science of Sweet + Heat

When you combine sugar and spice, your brain lights up like a Christmas tree. According to McGee (2004), sugar intensifies flavour perception while capsaicin (from chillies) stimulates the trigeminal nerve, basically your mouth's drama queen. Add texture, acid, or creaminess to the mix and you've just hacked into the reward circuits of your brain. It's dessert... with edge. Shepherd (2006) adds that multisensory experiences, like something being sweet, cold, crunchy, and spicy all at once, make flavour more memorable. So yes, when you serve a scoop of vanilla ice cream with hot chilli syrup, you're not being weird. You're being a genius.

VANILLA ICE CREAM WITH HOT CHILLI HONEY DRIZZLE

COLD, CREAMY, AND KISSED BY FIRE.

YIELD: SERVES 4 **HEAT LEVEL: 🌶 (WARM)**

INGREDIENTS:

- 1 good-quality vanilla ice cream
- 1/2 cup honey
- 1 small red chilli, thinly sliced (or 1/2 tsp chilli flakes)
- 1 tbsp lemon juice

METHOD:

1. In a small saucepan, combine the honey and sliced chilli. Warm over low heat for 5-7 minutes, allowing the chilli to infuse the honey. Do not boil.
2. Remove from heat and stir in the lemon juice.
3. Let the honey cool to room temperature. The chilli will continue to infuse as it sits.
4. Scoop vanilla ice cream into bowls and drizzle generously with the chilli honey.

POACHED PEARS WITH STAR ANISE & CHILLI SYRUP

ELEGANT, FRAGRANT, AND SUBTLY SPICY.

YIELD: SERVES 4

HEAT LEVEL: (WARM)

INGREDIENTS:

- 4 firm but ripe pears (e.g., Bosc or Williams), peeled
- 4 cups water
- 1 cup sugar
- 1 cinnamon stick
- 3 star anise
- 1 whole dried chilli
- Strips of zest from 1 orange
- Crème fraîche or vanilla yoghurt, to serve

METHOD:

1. In a saucepan just large enough to hold the pears, combine the water, sugar, cinnamon, star anise, dried chilli, and orange zest. Bring to a simmer, stirring to dissolve the sugar.

2. Add the peeled pears to the syrup. Place a circle of parchment paper directly on the surface to keep the pears submerged.

3. Simmer gently for 20-30 minutes, or until the pears are tender when pierced with a knife.

4. Remove the pears with a slotted spoon. Bring the syrup to a boil and reduce by half until slightly thickened.

5. Serve the pears warm or at room temperature with a spoonful of the syrup and a dollop of crème fraîche.

Prescott and Stevenson (1996) found that novelty and contrast in food, like cold/hot, sweet/spicy, soft/crunchy, trigger higher enjoyment scores. So yes, these aren't just desserts. They're performances.

Tips to Keep It Magical (Not Mayhem)

- Pick one chilli element only. Don't go wild. Subtlety is sexy.
- Let your base be familiar: vanilla, fruit, pastry, then add the twist.
- Think texture. Spicy syrup on something soft? Gold. Crunchy brittle with soft mousse? Unstoppable.

And the most important? Serve it with confidence. Even if it's just Tuesday. Even if you're in socks.

9 AROUND THE WORLD IN 8 CHILLIES

Passport? Optional. Appetite? Mandatory.

This chapter is for the curious, the adventurous, and those who read "mild" on a menu and laugh softly to themselves. We're about to travel across four continents, eight chillies, and more flavour than your tastebuds legally agreed to handle. And yes, you're coming with me. Bring your stretchy pants.

After sweet desserts snuck chillies into sorbets, snacks, and syrups, you'd think we were done. But oh no, my spicy soulmate. We're just getting started. Now, we leave the kitchen and go globe-hopping with a chilli lens: salsas in Mexico, chaats in India, green curry in Thailand, and the unapologetic heat of the American South.

Each country doesn't just use chillies; they romance them. Each with their own rules, rituals, and (occasionally suspicious) spice tolerance levels. This isn't about "one chilli fits all." This is about technique, culture, and the chilli's transformation from fiery villain to culinary legend.

You'll learn what makes each region's heat so unique, which chillies are used where, and how to bring those world flavours home without needing a visa, or a fire extinguisher.

First stop? Mexico, where chillies don't ask for permission. They show up in moles, margaritas, and miracles. Ready to salsa your way in? Let's go.

Mexico – Salsas, Moles & Margaritas

If chillies had a birthplace where they were raised on fire and flair, it'd be Mexico. This is the land where chillies don't just show up; they take the lead, hit the high notes, and salsa their way straight into your soul.

Step into a Mexican kitchen and you'll find chillies everywhere: dried, smoked, ground, toasted, soaked, stuffed, pickled, even sipped. They're the Lady Gaga of the pantry: bold, unforgettable, and never just a background vocalist. Always the headliner, never the opening act.

Coming off a world of sweet-heat desserts, you'd think it was time to chill. But here? Chillies get serious. We're diving into deep, complex sauces, sharp, fresh salsas, and cocktails that make your lips tingle and your heart shout, "One more!"

Meet the Power Players

Let's start with the core crew:

- **Ancho:** dried poblano, sweet and smoky like a roasted raisin with attitude
- **Guajillo:** bright red, medium heat, tastes like sunshine and spice
- **Pasilla:** dark, earthy, a bit fruity, your mole's best friend
- **Arbol:** fiery, punchy, and great in salsas (but respect it)

According to Bosland and Votava (2012), Mexican cuisine uses over 60 native varieties of chillies, each with unique heat profiles and flavour compounds. That's not a spice rack. That's a library.

Salsa: The National Love Language

Let's not pretend salsa is a condiment. In Mexico, it's a religion.

SALSA ROJA (CLASSIC RED)

THE VIBRANT, ESSENTIAL TABLE SAUCE FOR TACOS, EGGS, AND EVERYTHING IN BETWEEN.

YIELD: MAKES ABOUT 2 CUPS **HEAT LEVEL: 🌶🌶 (MEDIUM)**

INGREDIENTS:

- 4 medium tomatoes
- 1/2 white onion, cut into chunks
- 2 cloves garlic, unpeeled
- 2-3 dried chilli de arbol (or 1-2 guajillo chillies), stems and seeds removed
- 1/4 cup fresh coriander, chopped
- Juice of 1 lime
- Salt to taste

METHOD:

1. Heat a dry skillet over medium-high heat. Roast the tomatoes, onion chunks, and unpeeled garlic until charred in spots, about 8-10 minutes. Remove the garlic once softened.
2. In the same skillet, briefly toast the dried chillies for 30 seconds per side until fragrant.
3. Soak the toasted chillies in hot water for 10 minutes to soften.
4. Peel the garlic. Combine all ingredients (tomatoes, onion, garlic, soaked chillies, coriander, lime juice, salt) in a blender.
5. Blend until smooth or slightly chunky, as preferred. Taste and adjust seasoning.

SALSA VERDE

ZESTY, TANGY, AND PERFECT FOR CUTTING THROUGH RICH MEATS.

YIELD: MAKES ABOUT 1.5 CUPS **HEAT LEVEL: ❩❩ (MEDIUM)**

INGREDIENTS:

- 500g tomatillos, husks removed and rinsed
- 1-2 jalapeños or serrano chillies
- 1/2 white onion, chopped
- 1 clove garlic
- 1/4 cup fresh coriander, chopped
- Juice of 1 lime
- Salt to taste

METHOD:

1. Preheat a broiler/grill. Place the tomatillos and chillies on a baking sheet and broil for 5-7 minutes, turning once, until blistered and softened.
2. Combine the charred tomatillos and chillies with the onion, garlic, coriander, and lime juice in a blender.
3. Blend until desired consistency is reached. Season with salt to taste.

These aren't just sauces. They're flavour amplifiers, bringing brightness and bite to rich, often cheesy or meaty dishes. McGee (2004) explains that acidity (from lime or tomatillos) sharpens spice perception while taming heat. That's why salsa tastes "hotter" and more balanced than raw chilli alone.

Moles: Sauce Meets Symphony

Now we're talking culinary opera. Moles are long-simmered, deeply layered sauces made with spices, seeds, chocolate, and, you guessed it, chillies. Mole poblano might have 20+ ingredients, including ancho, pasilla, almonds, cinnamon, and cacao. It's thick. It's rich. It's the edible equivalent of a passionate ballad sung in a thunderstorm.

According to Shepherd (2006), flavour perception heightens when ingredients with different aromas and textures are cooked together over time. Which is why a bite of mole on slow-cooked chicken feels like a plot twist your mouth didn't see coming.

Margaritas with Muscle

Let's end with a party. A traditional lime margarita is already iconic, but add a chilli salt rim or a splash of jalapeño-infused tequila and suddenly, it's a vacation and a dare.

Quick trick: Rub the rim of your glass with lime, dip in a mix of sea salt + ground arbol or chipotle, then pour in your drink. Sip. Smirk. Repeat.

Real-Life Flashback

I once made a guajillo salsa for a taco night. It was smooth, earthy, and surprisingly mellow. My friend Marcus (who thinks black pepper is "edgy") loved it, until I casually mentioned it had three kinds of chillies. He blinked. "I've been lied to." He finished the bowl anyway.

India – Curries, Chaats, and Chilli Bites

If Mexico turned chillies into passion, India turned them into poetry—rhythmic, intense, layered, and likely to leave you weeping with joy (or capsaicin-induced eye sweat). In India, chillies don't just spice food. They orchestrate emotion. One dish can hit sweet, sour, spicy, crunchy, and tangy in a single bite, and somehow still feel like a love letter from someone who wants to emotionally challenge you.

Coming from Mexico's mole symphonies and salsa sprints, India turns up the complexity. It's a place where even street snacks have philosophical depth. You'll find chillies hanging from doors to ward off evil, floating in oils to flavour curries, and being stuffed, fried, pickled, and powdered into legends.

A Quick Spice Map

India's chilli game is a regional affair. Some highlights:

- **Kashmiri Chillies:** Mild, deep red, and famous for colour more than heat. Think beautiful without the drama.
- **Guntur Chillies (Andhra Pradesh):** Red, hot, and fearless. Handle with respect.
- **Bird's Eye Chillies (Northeast):** Tiny devils with napalm-level heat. Use sparingly or while making peace with your ancestors.

According to Bosland and Votava (2012), India is one of the largest consumers and producers of chillies globally, with thousands of tonnes dried, powdered, and shipped across the country each year. In short: it's not a garnish. It's a national treasure.

Curries: The Main Event

There's a reason "curry" has become a shorthand for "flavour bomb." But here's the thing: curry isn't one dish; it's a universe.

CHICKEN CHETTINAD

A FIERY, AROMATIC CLASSIC FROM TAMIL NADU.

YIELD: SERVES 4

HEAT LEVEL: 🌶🌶🌶 (HOT)

INGREDIENTS:

- 500g chicken, cut into pieces
- 2 tbsp vegetable oil
- 1 large onion, finely chopped
- 2 tomatoes, chopped
- For the Chettinad Masala Paste:
  - 8-10 dried red chillies (e.g., Guntur)
  - 1 tbsp coriander seeds
  - 1 tsp cumin seeds
  - 1 tsp fennel seeds
  - 1/2 tsp black peppercorns
  - 4 cloves garlic
  - 1 inch ginger, chopped
  - 2 tbsp grated coconut (fresh or desiccated)
  - 1 tsp poppy seeds (optional)
  - 2 tbsp water

METHOD:

1. To make the masala paste, dry roast the dried chillies, coriander seeds, cumin seeds, fennel seeds, and peppercorns in a pan until fragrant. Let cool.
2. Grind the roasted spices with the garlic, ginger, coconut, poppy seeds (if using), and water to form a smooth paste.
3. Heat oil in a large pot. Sauté the chopped onion until golden brown.
4. Add the ground masala paste and cook for 5 minutes until the oil begins to separate.
5. Add the chopped tomatoes and cook until they break down into a sauce.
6. Add the chicken pieces and stir to coat in the masala. Cook for 10 minutes
7. Add 1 cup of water, bring to a boil, then simmer covered for 20-25 minutes until the chicken is cooked through and the sauce is thick. Season with salt.

What ties them together? The oil-spice-chilli base. McGee (2004) explains that heating spices in fat releases lipid-soluble flavour compounds. That's why Indian curries smell so aromatic and taste like someone planned every bite with love and a bit of mischief.

Chaats: Street Food with an Attitude

If curries are a hug, chaats are a slap, in the best way. These snacky, crunchy, saucy dishes combine hot, cold, soft, crispy, spicy, tangy, and sweet in one glorious mess.

QUICK CHAAT-STYLE POTATO SALAD

A SIMPLIFIED VERSION OF THE STREET FOOD MAGIC.

YIELD: SERVES 4 AS A SNACK

HEAT LEVEL: 🌶🌶 (MEDIUM)

INGREDIENTS:

- 4 medium potatoes, boiled, peeled, and cubed
- 1/2 cup plain yoghurt, whisked
- 2 tbsp tamarind chutney
- 1 tbsp green coriander chutney
- 1/2 tsp chaat masala
- 1/4 tsp roasted cumin powder
- 1 fresh green chilli, finely chopped (optional)
- Sev (thin chickpea noodles) and chopped coriander for garnish

METHOD:

1. Arrange the boiled potato cubes in a serving bowl.
2. Drizzle with the whisked yoghurt, tamarind chutney, and green chutney.
3. Sprinkle with chaat masala, cumin powder, and fresh chilli (if using).
4. Garnish generously with sev and fresh coriander. Serve immediately

They're not fancy. They're not polite. They're addictive. And they use green chillies like punctuation marks in the language of snack seduction.

Chilli Bites to Write Home About

Mirchi Bajji: Whole chillies stuffed with spiced mashed potato or tamarind, dipped in chickpea flour, and fried. Yes, it's hot. Yes, it's worth it.

Thecha (Maharashtra): A raw paste of green chillies, garlic, and peanuts. Meant to be eaten with flatbreads and bravado.
Shepherd (2006) explains that chilli's burn triggers endorphin release. So technically, chaat-induced tears = culinary euphoria. Science says so.

Real-Life Flashback

I once made a simple chaat at home. Chopped cucumber, tomato, coriander, pomegranate, yoghurt, and one tiny green chilli. My friend Asha took a bite, paused, and said, "This tastes like summer had a scandal." She meant it as a compliment.

Thailand – Tangy, Sweet, and Fiery

This is the part where chilli stops whispering and starts dancing on the table in a coconut bra.

Welcome to Thailand. A place where sweet, sour, salty, spicy, and umami don't just coexist; they hook arms, take a shot of fish sauce, and waltz through your bloodstream like they own it. This isn't casual spice. This is controlled chaos served on a banana leaf, and chillies are absolutely in charge.

Coming straight from India's curry cathedrals and chaat carnivals, you might think you've seen it all. You haven't. Thai food doesn't play by the rules. It rewrites the recipe in red curry paste and sets your mouth on a tropical rollercoaster.

The Heat Hits Different Here

In Thai cuisine, chillies don't just "add heat." They balance sweetness. They cut through coconut. They slap sourness into submission. It's not about shock value. It's about harmony with bite.

The key players:

- **Bird's Eye Chilli (Prik Kee Noo):** Tiny. Vicious. Cute until it ruins your credibility.
- **Dried Red Chillies:** Smoky and warm. Used in oils and pastes like they're plotting something.
- **Chilli Jam (Nam Prik Pao):** Sticky, smoky, sweet, and spicy. Like if marmalade had secrets.

According to Bosland and Votava (2012), the heat of bird's eye chillies ranks around 100,000 SHU. That's roughly 50 times hotter than a jalapeño. And yet… Thai grannies stir it into porridge like it's no big deal. That's cultural power.

The Holy Trinity: Sweet. Sour. Spicy.

SOM TUM (GREEN PAPAYA SALAD)

CRUNCHY, TART, FUNKY, AND LACED WITH RAW CHILLI.

YIELD: SERVES 2-3 AS A SIDE **HEAT LEVEL:))) (HOT)**

INGREDIENTS:

- 1 cup shredded green papaya
- 2 long beans, cut into 2-inch lengths (or a handful of green beans)
- 2 cloves garlic
- 2-4 Thai bird's eye chillies (adjust to your bravery level)
- 2 tbsp roasted peanuts
- 4 cherry tomatoes, halved
- 1 tbsp dried shrimp (optional, for authenticity)
- 2 tbsp lime juice
- 1.5 tbsp fish sauce (or soy sauce for vegetarian)
- 1 tbsp palm sugar or brown sugar

METHOD:

1. Using a mortar and pestle, pound the garlic and chillies until broken down.
2. Add the long beans and peanuts. Lightly pound to bruise them.
3. Add the papaya, tomatoes, and dried shrimp (if using). Pound lightly to mix and bruise the ingredients.
4. Add the lime juice, fish sauce, and palm sugar. Use a spoon and the pestle to toss and mix everything together.
5. Taste and adjust the seasoning—it should be a balance of sour, salty, sweet, and spicy. Serve immediately.

THAI RED CURRY (GAENG DAENG)

A CREAMY, AROMATIC CURRY THAT BUILDS HEAT WITH EVERY SPOONFUL.

YIELD: SERVES 4

HEAT LEVEL: (MEDIUM)

INGREDIENTS:

- 1 tbsp vegetable oil
- 3-4 tbsp Thai red curry paste
- 400ml can coconut milk
- 500g chicken, beef, tofu, or vegetables, cut into bite-sized pieces
- 2 tbsp fish sauce (or soy sauce)
- 1 tbsp palm sugar or brown sugar
- 1 red bell pepper, sliced
- A handful of Thai basil leaves
- Juice of 1/2 lime

METHOD:

1. Heat the oil in a wok or large pan over medium heat. Add the curry paste and fry for 1-2 minutes until fragrant.
2. Add about a quarter of the thick coconut cream from the top of the can. Cook, stirring, for 2-3 minutes until the oil starts to separate..
3. Add your protein/vegetables and stir to coat in the paste. Cook for a few minutes
4. Pour in the remaining coconut milk and bring to a gentle simmer. Cook until the protein is cooked through and tender.
5. Stir in the fish sauce, sugar, and bell pepper. Simmer for another 5 minutes.
6. Remove from heat. Stir in the Thai basil and lime juice. Serve with jasmine rice.

According to Shepherd (2006), layering flavours (like Thai dishes do naturally) creates multisensory stimulation, increasing the emotional connection to food. That's why a Thai meal doesn't just feed you; it seduces you. Then politely leaves you sweating.

Real-Life Warning

One time in Chiang Mai, I ordered som tum from a market stall. The cook raised one eyebrow and asked, "How spicy?" I, full of tourist bravado, said,

"Thai spicy."

She paused. "You sure?"

I nodded.

She made it.

I cried publicly, drank three coconuts, and earned a thumbs-up from a child nearby. Worth it.

Southern U.S. – Cajun Heat & Nashville Fire

You thought Thailand was wild? Buckle your biscuits, sweetheart, we're headed to the American South. A place where chilli comes deep-fried, butter-soaked, cast-iron-seared, and unapologetically loud. Down here, heat is a handshake, a challenge, and sometimes a personality trait.

This isn't delicate heat. This isn't "maybe I'll taste the chilli if I focus." This is Cajun sass and Nashville revenge. This is chilli that struts into the room wearing cowboy boots and shouting "Bless your heart" while it torches your esophagus.

After Thailand's tangy complexity, the South kicks the door down and says: "Sugar, if it ain't crispy, creamy, or capable of ruining your mascara, we don't want it."

The Southern Heat Aesthetic

Let's set the mood:

- **Cayenne Pepper** – the backbone of Southern fire. Not flashy. Just lethal and loyal.
- **Tabasco Sauce** – aged, vinegary, and practically a condiment in baby bottles around here.
- **Hot Sauce Dust** – yes, that's a thing. Yes, people carry it in their purses.
- **Dry Rubs** – full of chilli powder, brown sugar, smoked paprika, and the Lord's will.

According to Bosland and Votava (2012), cayenne's capsaicin content ranges between 30,000–50,000 SHU, which is basically the chilli equivalent of a Southern grandma's glare. It burns, but you know it's because she loves you.

Cajun Cooking: Where Roux Meets Ruckus

Cajun food isn't subtle. It's not trying to impress you with plating or precision. It's here to feed your soul and scorch your tongue.

SIMPLE JAMBALAYA

IT'S LIKE PAELLA GOT INTO A BAR FIGHT.

YIELD: SERVES 6

HEAT LEVEL: (MEDIUM)

INGREDIENTS:

- 2 tbsp olive oil
- 400g andouille or other spicy sausage, sliced
- 1 large onion, chopped
- 1 green bell pepper, chopped
- 2 celery stalks, chopped
- 3 cloves garlic, minced
- 1 tbsp Cajun seasoning
- 1/2 tsp smoked paprika
- 1/4 tsp cayenne pepper (or to taste)
- 400g can crushed tomatoes
- 2 cups chicken stock
- 1.5 cups long-grain white rice, rinsed
- 300g raw prawns, peeled and deveined
- 2 spring onions, sliced
- Salt and black pepper to taste

METHOD:

1. Heat the oil in a large, heavy-based pot or Dutch oven over medium-high heat. Brown the sausage slices. Remove and set aside.
2. In the same pot, sauté the onion, bell pepper, and celery (the "holy trinity") until softened, about 5-7 minutes. Add the garlic and cook for 1 more minute.
3. Stir in the Cajun seasoning, smoked paprika, and cayenne. Cook for 30 seconds until fragrant.
4. Return the sausage to the pot. Add the crushed tomatoes, chicken stock, and rice. Season with salt and pepper. Bring to a boil.
5. Reduce heat to low, cover, and simmer for 20-25 minutes, until the rice is cooked and has absorbed most of the liquid.
6. Stir in the prawns, cover, and cook for another 5 minutes until the prawns are pink and cooked through.
7. Fluff with a fork, stir in the spring onions, and serve.

McGee (2004) notes that spices like cayenne become more aromatic when cooked in fat, which explains why these dishes feel both bold and buttery. It's not just fire; it's flavour you respect.

Nashville Hot Chicken: The Deep-Fried Dare

This dish deserves its own warning label. It's fried chicken dipped in spiced oil—yes, *after* it's already fried. Think cayenne sludge + lard + spite. According to Shepherd (2006), spicy food stimulates pain receptors that the brain often mistakes for pleasure. So yes, hot chicken hurts. But also yes, people keep eating it while crying and smiling like unhinged saints.

Real-life story? I once tried the "medium" version at Prince's Hot Chicken in Nashville. My tongue went numb. A stranger handed me a napkin. A man near me proposed to his girlfriend between bites. It was beautiful. And traumatic.

10 AFROCHILLI – HEAT FROM THE MOTHERLAND

"You can't understand a culture without tasting it." – James Beard

And now, my fellow spice explorer, we arrive at the mother of all chapters, the Motherland herself. After a round-the-world chilli tour that started with mole mischief, danced through curry chaos, flirted with Thai sweet heat, and got deep-fried in the Southern U.S., we land where chilli takes on soul, history, and swagger: Africa.

If the last chapters were chilli's nightclub tour, this one is its homecoming parade. It's drums, drums, and more drums, flavours that don't ask for attention but demand respect. This is heat that tells stories, has ancestors, and probably owns a goat.

And no, African spice doesn't just mean "hot." It means bold. It means layered. It means that aunty in the corner who adds "just a little" Scotch bonnet and watches you cry like you stubbed your emotions.

So buckle up. We're about to get saucy with Peri-Peri from Southern Africa, go deep into Harissa from the North, simmer through Scotch Bonnet stews from the West, and wrap it all in the golden crunch of East African samosas.

Hungry? Brave? Curious? Good. Let's kick it off with "Southern Africa – Peri-Peri Power."

Southern Africa – Peri-Peri Power

If chillies had a passport, Peri-Peri would have more stamps than a jet-setting pop star with a spicy entourage. From the coasts of Mozambique to the heart of South Africa, this sauce isn't just famous; it's a full-blown legend. The kind of condiment that walks into the room late, drenched in garlic and citrus, and still steals the show.

Now, you might've heard of Peri-Peri because of a certain fast-food chicken chain that rhymes with Bando's, but let me tell you: the real stuff? It's bolder. It's brasher. And it's been slapping taste buds long before "mild, hot, or extra hot?" was even a question.

Coming off our chilli-soaked adventures through Nashville firestorms and Thai citrus explosions, Southern Africa brings something different to the table. It's heat with heritage. Flavour with footwork. The chilli in these dishes isn't just spice; it's story.

The Peri-Peri Origin Story

Let's rewind. Portuguese traders brought the African bird's eye chilli to Mozambique centuries ago, and local cooks said, "Cute. Let's make it bite harder." What followed was Peri-Peri sauce, a fiery fusion of African chillies, garlic, vinegar, citrus, and oil.

According to Bosland and Votava (2012), the African bird's eye chilli (*Capsicum frutescens*) clocks in between 100,000 to 175,000 SHU. So yes, it's tiny. But also yes, it can humble even the most confident palate.

This sauce became a staple, brushed over chicken, mixed into marinades, splashed on seafood, and occasionally weaponised at family barbecues.

Real Talk: The Flavour Profile

Peri-Peri is:

- Spicy but not mindless.
- Acidic, thanks to lemon or vinegar.
- Rich from oil.
- Deeply garlicky.
- Slightly sweet (if you're fancy and add bell peppers or a splash of honey).

McGee (2004) explains that oil and acid don't just carry flavour; they amplify it. That's why Peri-Peri hits like a lemony flame that gets louder with each bite. It lingers. It builds. It never whispers.

PIRI-PIRI PRAWNS

QUICK, FIERY, AND PERFECT WITH CRUSTY BREAD FOR MOPPING UP THE SAUCE

YIELD: SERVES 2-3 **HEAT LEVEL:))) (HOT)**

INGREDIENTS:

- 500g large raw prawns, shell-on or peeled
- 3 tbsp Piri-Piri sauce (see below)
- 2 tbsp butter, melted
- 2 cloves garlic, minced
- Juice of 1/2 lemon
- Salt to taste
- Chopped parsley or coriander for garnish

METHOD:

1. In a bowl, combine the Piri-Peri sauce, melted butter, garlic, and lemon juice.

2. Add the prawns and toss to coat. Let marinate for 15-30 minutes.

3. Heat a grill pan or skillet over high heat. Cook the prawns for 1-2 minutes per side until pink and cooked through.

4. Garnish with fresh herbs and serve immediately with lemon wedges and bread.

HOMEMADE PIRI-PIRI SAUCE

MAKE YOUR OWN LEGENDARY SAUCE TO SLATHER ON EVERYTHING.

YIELD: MAKES ABOUT 1 CUP **HEAT LEVEL: (HOT)**

INGREDIENTS:

- 10-15 African bird's eye chillies (or other hot red chillies)
- 4 cloves garlic
- 1/2 cup olive oil
- 1/4 cup red wine vinegar
- Juice of 1 lemon
- 1 tsp smoked paprika
- 1 tsp dried oregano
- 1/2 tsp salt

METHOD:

1. Combine all ingredients in a blender or food processor.

2. Blend until a coarse or smooth paste forms, depending on your preference.

3. Transfer to a jar and let it sit for at least a few hours, preferably overnight, for the flavours to meld.

Shepherd (2006) confirms that the interplay between temperature, fat, and spice enhances flavour intensity, so grilling this sauce isn't just tradition. It's culinary science with fire emojis.

North African Harissa Heaven

If Peri-Peri is the lively cousin who throws backyard braais with a chilli-soaked apron and a beer in hand, then Harissa is the moody artist, all smoky glances, ancient spice secrets, and a long-term relationship with olive oil. Welcome to North Africa, where chillies don't rush. They simmer. They smoulder. And they arrive with depth, drama, and centuries of flavour behind them.

Coming off Southern Africa's Peri-Peri rave, Harissa enters like it's walking in slow motion through a sandstorm, wearing spice-stained robes and whispering in Arabic. It's not here to scream. It's here to haunt your tastebuds gently and seduce your leftovers for days.

What is Harissa, Anyway?

Let's get it straight: Harissa isn't just a chilli paste. It's an institution.
At its heart, Harissa is made of:

- Dried red chillies (often Baklouti or Guajillo-style)
- Garlic
- Olive oil
- Cumin
- Caraway
- Coriander
- Lemon juice or vinegar
- Salt

It's blended into a thick, red paste that looks innocent but hides a slow-building fire. According to Bosland and Votava (2012), dried Baklouti chillies sit between 4,000–5,000 SHU, but their complexity multiplies when toasted and blended with earthy spices.

In Tunisia, Morocco, and Algeria, Harissa is a fridge staple, a breakfast spread, a marinade, and, if you know an aunty who takes it seriously, a competitive sport.

Flavour Profile: Layered Like Desert Sand

Harissa isn't all about the heat. It's warm, not wild. The chillies provide a mellow burn that develops slowly, while spices bring smoky depth. Garlic sharpens it. Oil smooths it. Acid lifts it. It's like your favourite jazz record: low burn, high impact.

McGee (2004) explains that oil emulsifies capsaicin and essential oils in spices, allowing fat-soluble flavour compounds to disperse evenly and linger longer. That's why a spoon of Harissa on roasted veg tastes more intense after the second bite. It grows on you. Then clings lovingly to your tongue like an overenthusiastic ex.

HARISSA-ROASTED CARROTS WITH YOGHURT

A SIMPLE SIDE THAT STEALS THE SHOW.

YIELD: SERVES 4 AS A SIDE **HEAT LEVEL: 🌶🌶🌶 (MEDIUM)**

INGREDIENTS:

- 500g carrots, peeled and cut into batons
- 2 tbsp olive oil
- 1-2 tbsp harissa paste
- Salt and black pepper
- To serve: 1/2 cup Greek yoghurt, 1 tbsp lemon juice, chopped mint or parsley

METHOD:

1. Preheat oven to 200°C (400°F).
2. In a bowl, toss the carrot batons with olive oil, harissa paste, salt, and pepper until evenly coated.
3. Spread on a baking sheet and roast for 25-30 minutes, until tender and caramelised at the edges.
4. While the carrots roast, mix the Greek yoghurt with lemon juice and a pinch of salt.
5. Spread the yoghurt on a serving plate, top with the roasted carrots, and garnish with fresh herbs.

Flashback

I once served harissa-roasted carrots at a dinner party. Just carrots. With yoghurt. No one shut up about them for hours. People took photos. A guy asked for the recipe like it was state intel. I said, "I rubbed them in harissa and roasted them." He blinked. "That's it?" I nodded. He married someone else, but I know he still thinks about those carrots.

West African Scotch Bonnet Stews

Now listen, if Harissa was the slow-burning seductress, then West Africa is the full-blown fire dancer with rhythm in her bones and a Scotch Bonnet in her purse. You've made it to the bold, the rich, the unapologetically fiery realm of West African cuisine, where chillies don't knock politely… they kick the door in with ancestral confidence.

Coming from the smoky depths of North Africa's harissa havens, West Africa greets you with big pots, bigger flavours, and chillies that bring both trauma and triumph. Here, food doesn't whisper. It sings. It preaches. It holds your tastebuds in a headlock, says a quick prayer, and then sets them free, stronger, bolder, and slightly singed.

The Star: The Scotch Bonnet Chilli

This little chilli might look like a citrusy ornament but don't be fooled. It's the Rihanna of the chilli world—sweet, vibrant, and powerful enough to shut down weak palates without even trying.

Scotch Bonnets rank between 100,000 and 350,000 SHU on the Scoville scale (Bosland & Votava, 2012). That's hotter than most habaneros, but here's the twist: they come with a tropical, almost fruity undertone that makes West African dishes taste like fire and sunshine had a baby.

Why the Heat Works So Well

West African stews are built for boldness. You've got:

- Base aromatics: onion, garlic, ginger
- Deep richness from: tomatoes, palm oil, stock
- Protein: goat, chicken, fish, beans, whatever's walking
- And then… the Scotch Bonnet. Blended right in. No mercy.

McGee (2004) explains that capsaicin bonds with the tongue's pain receptors and builds heat over time, exactly why your first spoon of Nigerian stew feels safe… until it doesn't. But that's the point. The burn is part of the beauty.

NIGERIAN TOMATO STEW (OBE ATA)

A RICH, VERSATILE BASE FOR COUNTLESS WEST AFRICAN DISHES.

YIELD: SERVES 4-6 **HEAT LEVEL: 🌶🌶🌶 (HOT)**

INGREDIENTS:

- 4 large red bell peppers, deseeded and chopped
- 2 large onions, chopped
- 4-6 Scotch Bonnet chillies, stems removed (adjust to taste)
- 400g can tomato puree
- 1/2 cup red palm oil
- 500g chicken, beef, or fish, cooked and shredded (optional)
- 1 tbsp curry powder
- 2 stock cubes
- Salt to taste

METHOD:

1. Blend the bell peppers, onions, and Scotch Bonnet chillies with a little water until smooth.
2. Heat the palm oil in a large pot over medium heat. Be careful not to overheat it.
3. Carefully add the blended pepper mixture to the hot oil. It will splatter. Stir and fry for 20-25 minutes, until the mixture darkens and the oil separates and floats to the top.
4. Stir in the tomato puree and cook for another 10 minutes.
5. Add the curry powder, stock cubes, and salt. Stir well.
6. If using, add your pre-cooked protein and simmer for 10 minutes to heat through and allow the flavours to meld. Serve with rice, plantains, or beans.

Shepherd (2006) points out that heat triggers endorphin release, making the brain associate pain with pleasure, which explains why we go back for second helpings while still sweating.

Real-Life Flashback
My Nigerian aunt once made tomato stew with two Scotch bonnets "just for flavour." My cousin took one bite, stood up, and walked into the garden to stare at a tree. He didn't speak for twenty minutes. When he came back, he said, "That was divine. I saw my future." I knew exactly what he meant.

East African Samosas with Kick

If you made it this far, I just want to say: you deserve a standing ovation, a glass of cold mango juice, and a samosa that doesn't betray you. But that's not the samosa we're talking about today. No, no, we're talking about *that* samosa. The one with the innocent triangle shape, golden crisp edges, and a smile on its face that says, "Go on, take a bite. I dare you."

Welcome to East Africa, where Indian influence met African ingenuity, and chillies were folded, literally, into flaky pastry parcels like well-hidden scandal. This isn't your office party samosa. This is a crunchy uppercut wrapped in dough.

Coming straight out of Scotch Bonnet stewland, you might think, "How bad can a little pastry be?" That's cute. That's adorable. East African samosas don't ask questions. They serve vibes, flavour, and just the right amount of existential crisis.

The Anatomy of a Samosa (with Motive)
Let's break it down:

- Thin, flaky pastry, innocent exterior
- Spiced meat, potatoes, lentils, or veg, the plotline
- Fresh chilli, garlic, and onion, the betrayal
- Deep-fried until it crackles like your mum's mood when you say "I'm full"

The chilli? Usually green bird's eye or serrano. It's chopped finely, tucked inside like a spy with good cheekbones, and left there to ambush you mid-chew.
Bosland and Votava (2012) describe bird's eye chillies as reaching up to 100,000 SHU. Translation? Don't trust anything cute and green in this region unless it's cash.

Flavour Profile: Crunch, Boom, Ah!

One bite = flaky crunch.

Second bite = oh, warm potatoes and cumin.

Third bite = wait… why is my tongue sweating?

That's the East African samosa arc. It builds. It charms. Then it unleashes flavour like a choir of spiced gremlins. And yes, I mean that as a compliment. McGee (2004) explains that heat is perceived more strongly when paired with fats and starches, so when you put chilli inside oily, carby pastry, you've basically built a spice delivery rocket. And oh, it launches.

SPICED BEEF SAMOSAS

THE ULTIMATE SAVOURY, SPICY, CRUNCHY HAND-HELD SNACK.

YIELD: MAKES 12-15 SAMOSAS

HEAT LEVEL:)) (MEDIUM)

INGREDIENTS:

- 1 packet spring roll pastry or samosa pastry (about 15 sheets)
- 2 tbsp oil
- 1 small onion, finely chopped
- 2 cloves garlic, minced
- 1 tsp fresh ginger, grated
- 1-2 green chillies, finely chopped
- 250g beef mince
- 1 tsp ground cumin
- 1 tsp ground coriander
- 1/2 tsp turmeric
- 1 tbsp lemon juice
- 2 tbsp fresh coriander, chopped
- Salt and pepper to taste
- Oil for deep or shallow frying

METHOD:

1. Heat the oil in a pan over medium heat. Sauté the onion until soft. Add garlic, ginger, and green chilli; cook for 1 minute.

2. Add the beef mince and cook until browned, breaking it up with a spoon.

3. Stir in the cumin, coriander, turmeric, salt, and pepper. Cook for 2 minutes. Stir in lemon juice and fresh coriander. Let the filling cool completely.

4. Cut the spring roll sheets in half lengthwise. Fold each strip into a cone shape, fill with a teaspoon of filling, then fold over to seal into a triangle. Use a paste of flour and water to seal the edges.

5. Heat oil in a deep pan to 180°C (350°F). Fry the samosas in batches until golden brown and crisp. Drain on paper towels.

According to Shepherd (2006), multisensory combinations—crunch, fat, spice, and heat—trigger pleasure responses in the brain even as the body screams "WHYYYYY."

Real-Life Flashback

My cousin once brought samosas to a family picnic. No label. No warning. Just a pretty tray with napkins. My uncle, who once described "mild salsa" as "a bit sharp," grabbed three. After bite two, he was fanning himself with a paper plate and singing gospel. He recovered. But he still side-eyes anything triangular.

11 THE SPICE OF ASIA

"You don't need a silver fork to eat good food." – Paul Prudhomme

Now, Paul was probably standing in a Louisiana kitchen when he said that, but if he'd ever tasted a Thai curry or dipped a rice roll into sambal with trembling fingers, he'd have nodded with extra conviction. Asia doesn't serve spice with politeness. No. It slaps it onto the plate like it's breaking up with your taste buds… and oddly, you'll keep coming back for more.

In the last chapter, we danced through the bold beats of Africa's chilli-soaked roots, from peri-peri drums to scotch bonnet stews that made even the brave blink twice. But now, we're heading east, into a region where spice doesn't scream, it sings. Gochujang whispers its slow-burn secrets. Sichuan peppercorns flirt with your nerves like a dare. And birds' eye chillies? They don't ask for permission.

Get ready. Because Asia doesn't just cook. Asia seduces.

Korea – Gochujang Goodness

Before we dive into the thick, red, fermented beauty that is gochujang, let me say this: Korea didn't come to play. This isn't just heat. It's fermented fire with a PhD in flavor. Gochujang is the type of chilli paste that doesn't shout; it studies you. Then it ambushes your tongue like a K-drama plot twist you never saw coming.

So, what exactly is it? Gochujang is a fermented chilli paste made from red chilli powder, glutinous rice, fermented soybeans, and salt. It's deep, savory, and laced with a sweetness that sneaks up on you like your mum's passive-aggressive compliments. It's the backbone of bibimbap, the soul of tteokbokki, and the secret behind that addictively spicy fried chicken you pretend not to crave every other Wednesday night.

Let me tell you a quick story. I once tried making gochujang from scratch. I had dreams of mastery, ancestral kitchen vibes, and humble-brag Instagram posts. Two days in, my kitchen smelled like a spicy science experiment and my neighbors asked if I was storing old gym socks in soy sauce. Lesson? Buy the good stuff from the Korean aisle and keep your dignity.

Why It's Genius

Gochujang works because it's layered. It hits sweet, salty, umami, and spicy all at once. It's not the kind of spice that karate-kicks your throat. It's the one that builds quietly, like a nosy aunt, until it owns the conversation.
Even better, it's a team player. Mix it with sesame oil, and you've got a dressing. Toss it in mayo, and suddenly your sandwich thinks it's in Seoul. Stir it into soups? That's the culinary equivalent of handing your dish a mic and letting it belt high notes.

How to Use It Without Crying (Much)

If you're new to the Korean spice game, start small. A teaspoon in your stir-fry. A dollop on your rice bowl. Then work your way up like you're training for a spice triathlon. Pair it with honey or sugar to mellow the edges—trust me, sweet and heat are basically K-pop's spicy cousins.

GOCHUJANG GLAZED CAULIFLOWER

LIKE BUFFALO WINGS BUT SMARTER. AND REDDER. AND WITH FEWER REGRETS.

YIELD: SERVES 4 AS A SIDE **HEAT LEVEL: (MEDIUM)**

INGREDIENTS:

- 1 large head of cauliflower, cut into florets
- 2 tbsp gochujang
- 1 tbsp soy sauce
- 1 tbsp rice vinegar
- 1 tbsp maple syrup or honey
- 1 tbsp sesame oil
- 2 cloves garlic, minced
- 1 tsp fresh ginger, grated
- Toasted sesame seeds and spring onion for garnish

METHOD:

1. Preheat oven to 220°C (425°F).
2. In a large bowl, whisk together the gochujang, soy sauce, rice vinegar, maple syrup, sesame oil, garlic, and ginger.
3. Add the cauliflower florets and toss until evenly coated.
4. Spread on a baking sheet and roast for 20-25 minutes, until tender and caramelised at the edges.
5. Garnish with toasted sesame seeds and sliced spring onion

Fun fact: Gochujang is so iconic that South Korea actually designated it as a cultural heritage food (Korea Food Promotion Institute, 2020). That's right. They knighted a condiment. And I fully support it.

China – Sichuan and the Numbing Burn

"Some like it hot. But Sichuan? Sichuan likes it unapologetically volcanic, with a side of tongue-numbing wizardry."

You thought gochujang was bold? Buckle your seatbelt, friend. Because now we're heading into the smoky, pepper-punched world of Sichuan cuisine, where flavour doesn't knock, it breaks the door down and laughs while your mouth begs for mercy.

Let me introduce you to *mala*, the dynamic duo of *ma* (numbing) and *la* (spicy). It's a combo made in the fiery depths of food heaven. The numbing sensation comes from Sichuan peppercorns, which aren't actually peppers at all, but citrusy little devils that tingle your tongue like you just licked a 9-volt battery. And then comes the *la*, hot red chillies, fried in oil until they whisper terrifying things to your tastebuds.

I Tried Mala Hotpot Once…

I was feeling brave. The kind of brave that convinces you you're a spice warrior just because you survived a jalapeño once in college. So, I dunked my tofu, beef, mushrooms, the whole gang, into a bubbling red bath of chilli oil and peppercorns. Ten seconds in? My face went numb, my soul left my body, and I experienced an out-of-body hotness that made me question all my life choices. And yet… it was amazing.

The Science of the Burn

Sichuan peppercorns contain hydroxy-alpha-sanshool (try saying that three times fast), a compound that activates touch sensors instead of taste buds, creating that buzzing, lip-tingling sensation (Bryant & Mezine, 2021).

Combine that with capsaicin-packed chillies, and you've got a neurological rollercoaster that turns your face into a carnival ride.

And don't be fooled, Sichuan cuisine isn't just spice for the sake of spice. There's balance. There's finesse. There's the occasional sweet whisper behind the punch. Dishes like Kung Pao Chicken, Mapo Tofu, and Hot and Sour Soup showcase a dazzling choreography of spicy, sour, sweet, salty, and umami. It's like a five-member boy band where every member has main-character energy.

MAPO TOFU (SIMPLIFIED)

THIS DISH WILL MAKE TOFU FEEL DANGEROUS.

YIELD: SERVES 4

HEAT LEVEL:))) (HOT)

INGREDIENTS:

- 1 packet (450g) soft or firm tofu, cut into cubes
- 2 tbsp Sichuan chilli bean paste (Doubanjiang)
- 1 tbsp fermented black beans, rinsed and chopped
- 2 tsp Sichuan peppercorns, lightly crushed
- 3 cloves garlic, minced
- 1 tsp fresh ginger, grated
- 200g pork mince (optional, can be omitted for vegetarian)
- 1 cup vegetable or chicken stock
- 1 tbsp soy sauce
- 1 tsp sugar
- 2 spring onions, sliced
- 1 tbsp cornflour mixed with 2 tbsp water (slurry)

METHOD:

1. Blanch the tofu cubes in lightly salted boiling water for 2 minutes. Drain and set aside. This helps it hold its shape.

2. Heat a wok over medium-high heat. Add 2 tbsp oil. Add the Sichuan peppercorns and fry for 30 seconds until fragrant. Remove the peppercorns with a slotted spoon, leaving the infused oil.

3. Add the chilli bean paste to the oil and fry for 1 minute until the oil turns red. Add garlic and ginger; fry for 30 seconds.

4. If using, add the pork mince and break it up. Cook until no longer pink.

5. Pour in the stock, soy sauce, and sugar. Bring to a simmer.

6. Gently add the tofu cubes. Simmer for 5 minutes.

7. Stir the cornflour slurry and add it to the wok, stirring gently until the sauce thickens.

8. Garnish with spring onions and the reserved fried Sichuan peppercorns. Serve with steamed rice.

Want to Try It? Here's How to Dip In:

- Start with Kung Pao Chicken. It's the gateway drug. Slightly sweet, mildly spicy, and blessed with roasted peanuts for crunch.
- Level up to Mapo Tofu. This dish will make tofu feel dangerous. Silken cubes swimming in a lava of fermented bean paste, garlic, and enough chilli oil to power a small engine.
- Ready for glory? Try Sichuan Hotpot. But bring a sweat towel, a dairy chaser, and possibly a will.

Now that your mouth's tingling and your sinuses are clearer than your conscience after tax season, we're heading to a tropical archipelago where spice takes a saucier turn.

Indonesia – Sambal Sorcery

You survived Sichuan's fire and fury. You've battled mala and lived to tell the tale. Bravo. Now, take a deep breath—not too deep, though—because we're headed straight into the lush, spice-slicked jungles of Indonesia, where sambal reigns like a spicy queen with 257 personalities.

As Anthony Bourdain once said, "You don't truly know a country until you've eaten its street food." In Indonesia, that means facing sambal, a condiment, a sauce, a threat, and a love letter all rolled into one.

Let me say this loud and clear: sambal is not ketchup with a kick. It's not your supermarket's weak attempt at "spicy tomato dip." It is an ancient, tongue-waking ritual. And here's the fun part, there are over 200 variations, each with a local twist, attitude, and sometimes a sassy backstory.

Meet the Hot-Headed Legends

- **Sambal Terasi:** A punch of red chillies and fermented shrimp paste. Smells like old secrets. Tastes like a spicy dare.
- **Sambal Matah:** A Balinese masterpiece made with raw shallots, lemongrass, lime leaves, and chillies, like salsa that studied abroad and came back evolved.
- **Sambal Ijo:** Green chillies meet green tomatoes. Don't let the colour fool you. It's a sneaky one, like a polite person with mafia connections.

Each sambal type isn't just a recipe; it's a flavour memoir, a spicy diary entry written in oil, acid, and fire.

Real Talk: I Tried Making Sambal Once

Picture this: It's me, in my tiny kitchen, grinding red chillies, garlic, and terasi in a mortar and pestle like I'm on MasterChef: The Masochist Edition.

Thirty seconds in, my eyes are watering. Not from emotion, from the sheer chilli fumes clouding my vision like a bad decision.

I accidentally touched my nose, then my cheek. Rookie move. Let's just say, I spent the next hour fanning my own face like a Victorian widow. But that sambal? Worth every tear. It made boiled eggs taste like treasure, and plain rice felt like a VIP dish.

Sambal Science 101

Why does sambal hit different? It's not just heat. It's layered intensity. Sambal combines:

- Capsaicin (from the chillies), which we know lights up your nervous system like disco lights (Prescott & Stevenson, 2020).
- Umami depth from shrimp paste or anchovies.
- Acidic balance from lime or tamarind.
- Aromatic punch from garlic, lemongrass, shallots.

This is culinary alchemy. You're not just eating; you're activating neurons.

SAMBAL MATAH (BALINESE RAW SAMBAL)

FRESH, FRAGRANT, AND EXPLOSIVELY FLAVOURFUL.

YIELD: MAKES ABOUT 1 CUP **HEAT LEVEL: 🌶🌶 (MEDIUM)**

INGREDIENTS:

- 8-10 shallots, thinly sliced
- 4-6 Thai bird's eye chillies, thinly sliced
- 2 lemongrass stalks, tender white part only, very finely sliced
- 4 kaffir lime leaves, deveined and very finely shredded
- 1/4 tsp shrimp paste (terasi), toasted (optional)
- 3 tbsp hot coconut or neutral oil
- 2 tbsp lime juice
- Salt to taste

METHOD:

1. Combine the sliced shallots, chillies, lemongrass, and lime leaves in a heatproof bowl.
2. If using, mash the toasted shrimp paste with the back of a spoon and add it to the bowl.
3. Heat the oil in a small pan until very hot but not smoking.
4. Carefully pour the hot oil over the shallot and chilli mixture. It will sizzle and wilt the ingredients slightly.
5. Stir in the lime juice and salt to taste. Let it sit for 10 minutes for the flavours to meld before serving. Perfect with grilled fish or chicken.

How to Ease Into the Madness

If you're new to sambal, start gentle. Use it as a condiment with fried rice (Nasi Goreng), grilled chicken (Ayam Bakar), or eggs. Mix it into mayo for a spicy spread. Or just keep a tiny dollop on your plate like a fiery pet watching your every move.

You can even find sambal in jars now, but the homemade stuff? That's where the real magic brews. Like grandma's chilli potion passed down through generations of brave tastebuds.

And now that you've been anointed by the chilli gods of Indonesia, we head east again. You better tighten your seatbelt (or apron), because our next culinary journey lands smack between lime juice and fish sauce—welcome to Thailand & Vietnam – Birds' Eye Royalty. You ready, spice scout? Let's roll.

Thailand & Vietnam – Birds' Eye Royalty

Third-Person Storytelling with Heat, Humour & Facts

In a small street tucked behind Bangkok's bustling Chatuchak Market, a woman named Noi stirred a bowl of som tum papaya salad like she was conjuring a thunderstorm. She was 62, barefoot, and legendary. People didn't line up for her salad because of the crunch; they came for her chillies. Specifically, the *prik kee noo*, Thailand's infamous bird's eye chilli, tiny enough to look innocent but angry enough to slap your soul sideways.

Tourists called her "The Chilli Whisperer." Locals just called her "Ma Noi," and they knew better than to ask for extra spicy unless they were emotionally prepared for a life review. Every lunchtime, brave souls from around the globe gathered, watched her toss those deadly red daggers into her mortar, and made peace with their gastrointestinal system.

That's what made her salads sacred. Not the shredded papaya. Not the fish sauce. But those chillies, little firecrackers of Southeast Asia.

The Bird's Eye Bloodline

Whether you're in Thailand or Vietnam, the *Capsicum frutescens* family reigns like a royal dynasty, small in stature, massive in legacy. In Thai, they're called *prik kee noo suan* ("mouse-dropping chillies"), which sounds gross until you try one and realize it kicks like a Muay Thai champion on espresso.

In Vietnam, they go by *ớt hiểm*, and they're slipped into everything: fish sauce, pho, and sauces served with grilled meats. These chillies aren't blended; they're infused. Like gossip in a small town, once they're in, everything changes.

A Tale from Hanoi: Grandma Dung's Sauce

In Hanoi, there's another chilli matriarch: Grandma Dung. A retired

teacher with a passion for balance, she created a fish sauce blend so potent it made her son-in-law cry, and then ask for seconds.
Her secret?

- Bird's eye chillies
- Fresh lime juice
- Garlic slices
- A whisper of sugar
- And *nước mắm*, the Vietnamese fish sauce with a smell so bold it could evict your upstairs neighbor.

Locals would joke, "If you haven't sweated while eating Grandma Dung's dipping sauce, are you even Vietnamese?"

The Science Behind the Royalty

These chillies aren't just spicy for drama. Their heat sits around 100,000 Scoville units, that's 20x hotter than a jalapeño (Bosland & Votava, 2012). But it's not just about pain. The magic is in how they balance sweetness, saltiness, sourness, and umami. Thai and Vietnamese cuisines aren't shy; they layer flavours like a DJ layering bass lines—bold, rhythmic, and unforgettable.

In fact, *prik kee noo* and *ớt hiểm* contain high levels of capsaicin, known not only for the burn, but also for stimulating endorphins and improving metabolism (Ludy et al., 2012). Pain with benefits? Now we're talking.

VIETNAMESE NUOC CHAM DIPPING SAUCE

THE PERFECT BALANCE OF SWEET, SOUR, SALTY, AND FIERY HEAT

YIELD: MAKES ABOUT 1 CUP **HEAT LEVEL: 🌶🌶 (ADJUSTABLE)**

INGREDIENTS:

- 3 tbsp fish sauce
- 2 tbsp lime juice
- 3 tbsp sugar
- 1/4 cup warm water
- 1-2 Thai bird's eye chillies, thinly sliced
- 1 clove garlic, minced (optional)

METHOD:

1. In a small bowl, whisk the sugar with the warm water until dissolved.
2. Add the fish sauce and lime juice, and whisk to combine.
3. Stir in the sliced chillies and minced garlic (if using).
4. Let it sit for at least 15 minutes before serving to allow the flavours to meld. Serve as a dipping sauce for spring rolls, grilled meats, or drizzle over rice.

So next time you see a tiny red chilli staring up from your bowl in Bangkok or Hanoi, don't underestimate it. That's not a garnish. That's a royal decree. One bite, and you'll swear it shouted, "Bow before me!"

Now that Asia has treated us with both slap and song, it's time to ask: what's next when the flame calms and the heart wants to heal? Ah yes... Chapter 12 is coming. Where fire meets legacy. See you there, spice knight

.

12 AMERICAN HEATWAVES

"Americans will eat anything, so long as there's cheese and fire involved." – Probably someone's Texan grandma.

First of all, thank you for surviving 11 chapters of spice, sass, and global chilli diplomacy. If your tongue hasn't packed its bags and fled your mouth by now, you, my friend, are a certified heat seeker. And if you have taken a break to lie face-down on a cold tile floor? Respect. Been there. No judgement.

From Africa's scorching Scotch bonnets to Asia's mischievous Birds' Eye, we've trotted the globe like a hot sauce-crazed Phileas Fogg. But now, now we're touching down where chilli meets swagger, showbiz, and a Super Bowl halftime snack board. Yep, welcome to the land of fireworks in your nachos and drama in your barbecue: the good ol' U.S. of A.

But don't get it twisted. American heat isn't just about volume or violence. It's about vibe. It's cornbread cuddling up to cayenne. It's jalapeños stuffed with dreams and cheese. It's butter-soaked rebellion with a splash of Tabasco.

And I know what you're thinking: Can chilli really make a Tex-Mex meat stew taste like a six-hour nap in a cowboy hat? Yes. Yes it can. Let's begin.

Tex-Mex Tingle: Chilli Con Carne

Before we jump headfirst into this cowboy cauldron of glory, let me tell you a secret. Once, at a cook-off in Austin, I met a man who claimed his chilli recipe was so good it made his ex-wife come back, for the Tupperware. That, my friend, is the power of chilli con carne. It brings people together… and then burns their taste buds into submission.

Let’s get our boots muddy in the land of Tex-Mex, where cowboys don't cry, unless the jalapeños say so.

Chilli con carne literally means “chilli with meat,” but that’s like saying a Ferrari is “a car with wheels.” This stew is the poster child of American spice, equal parts beefy bravado, simmered secrets, and a slow burn that whispers, *I’m here for a good time, not a bland time.*

Now, let’s build it right. You start with beef, preferably chuck, because ground beef alone is like a cowboy without a hat. Add some onions, garlic, and a trio of chillies: smoky ancho, spicy jalapeño, and rebellious chipotle. Then, pour in crushed tomatoes like you're apologizing to your ancestors for every bland meal you ever ate. Finish it off with cumin, smoked paprika, and a whisper of cocoa powder. Yes, cocoa. It’s not dessert. It’s depth.

Don’t even ask about beans. In Texas, adding beans to chilli is how bar fights start. Personally, I say follow your heart, but don’t tell a Texan I said that.

TEXAS-STYLE CHILLI CON CARNE (NO BEANS)

A RICH, SMOKY, AND DEEPLY SATISFYING BOWL OF RED.

YIELD: SERVES 6-8

HEAT LEVEL: (MEDIUM)

INGREDIENTS:

- 2 tbsp vegetable oil
- 1.5 kg beef chuck, cut into 2cm cubes
- 1 large onion, chopped
- 4 cloves garlic, minced
- 2-3 dried ancho chillies, stems and seeds removed
- 2-3 dried chipotle chillies, stems and seeds removed
- 2 fresh jalapeños, finely chopped
- 2 tbsp ground cumin
- 1 tbsp smoked paprika
- 1 tsp dried oregano
- 1 tbsp cocoa powder
- 800g can crushed tomatoes
- 4 cups beef stock
- Salt and black pepper to taste
- To serve: sour cream, shredded cheese, chopped coriander, diced onion

METHOD:

1. Tear the dried ancho and chipotle chillies into pieces. Cover with boiling water and soak for 20 minutes until soft. Blend into a smooth paste.

2. Pat the beef dry and season generously with salt and pepper. Heat the oil in a large, heavy-based pot or Dutch oven over medium-high heat and brown the beef in batches. Set aside.

3. In the same pot, sauté the onion until soft, about 5-7 minutes. Add the garlic and chopped jalapeños; cook for 1 minute.

4. Add the cumin, smoked paprika, and oregano; cook for 30 seconds until fragrant.

5. Return the beef to the pot. Stir in the chilli paste, crushed tomatoes, beef stock, and cocoa powder. Bring to a boil.

6. Reduce heat to low, cover, and simmer gently for 2.5 - 3 hours, until the beef is fork-tender. Season with salt and pepper to taste.

7. Serve with your choice of toppings like sour cream, shredded cheese, fresh coriander, and diced onion.

Let's spice things up with some cultural seasoning:

- According to the International Chili Society (yes, that's a real thing), the first chili cook-off was held in 1967 in Terlingua, Texas. It ended in a tie and a shouting match. Classic. (International Chili Society, 2021)
- Historian Frank X. Tolbert once called chili "a bowl of blessed hell," and honestly, what better endorsement could you ask for? (Tolbert, *A Bowl of Red*, 1966)
- A 2020 TasteAtlas survey ranked Texan chilli con carne among the top 10 comfort foods in North America. Probably helped by the fact that it doubles as both food and fire hazard. (TasteAtlas, 2020)

We've conquered the meat volcano. But don't wipe your mouth yet. Up next: Buffalo Wings & Blue Cheese, aka the unofficial currency of American sports bars. Shall we?

Buffalo Wings & Blue Cheese: The Tinder Date That Ended in Fire and Dairy

They say opposites attract. But whoever first dunked a lava-hot, cayenne-coated chicken wing into a bowl of cooling blue cheese didn't just prove that theory, they married it, gave it three kids, and sent it to culinary therapy. Welcome to Buffalo Wings & Blue Cheese: the Romeo and Juliet of American spice stories. Except in this case, nobody dies... unless you count the chicken.

Now, before I take you to the messiest finger-lickin' section of this chapter, let me remind you where we've just strutted from. In the last section, we flirted with Tex-Mex, an unapologetic riot of cumin and chilli that made your kitchen smell like a mariachi band having a midlife crisis. But now, we're heading northeast, to a tiny corner of New York where one late-night bar experiment birthed a global wing phenomenon that somehow became the official food of sports, manhood, and poorly planned bachelor parties.

Let's set the scene.

The Accidental Flame

It's 1964. Anchor Bar, Buffalo, New York. Teressa Bellissimo is in the kitchen when her son and his rowdy college friends show up unannounced. With nothing but leftover chicken wings (which were usually reserved for stock or the trash), she tosses them in hot sauce and butter, fries them till golden, and serves them with a bowl of blue cheese and celery sticks to cool the flames.

Boom. The world changed. And so did how we feel about napkins.
To this day, I can't eat Buffalo wings without feeling like I'm in a food duel with destiny. You too, right? The kind where your lips burn, your nose drips,

but you power through because quitting is for people who use forks to eat pizza.

The Sauce Matters, and So Does the Sweat

Not all Buffalo sauces are made equal. A real one is a slick blend of Frank's RedHot (accept no substitutes), butter, vinegar, and a touch of garlic powder. That's it. No sugar. No ketchup. No fancy stuff. The goal isn't to make it sweet, it's to make it sting, seduce, and smack you around a little. And that blue cheese dressing? It's not just a dip. It's your wingman. Literally. The creamy, tangy coolness isn't an afterthought; it's the necessary balm to your poultry pain. Without it, Buffalo wings are like breakdancing without kneepads. Bold, but stupid.

Wings in the Wild

Let me tell you about this guy I met at a summer BBQ once, Trevor. Stockbroker by day, hot sauce addict by destiny. He entered a wing-eating contest for charity, thinking he had the stomach of a dragon. He didn't. By wing twelve, his glasses were fogged, his lips looked like someone had stenciled them with red marker, and he kept muttering, "It's just residual heat, it's fine, I'm fine." Long story short: he now only eats cucumber sandwiches and has mild PTSD whenever he hears the word "Buffalo."

But Trevor's sacrifice taught us a lesson: Buffalo wings are not a game. They're a right of passage. And you, my friend, are ready for the initiation.

CLASSIC BUFFALO WINGS WITH BLUE CHEESE DIP

THE ULTIMATE PARTY FOOD THAT DEMANDS A STACK OF NAPKINS

YIELD: SERVES 4 AS A MAIN

HEAT LEVEL: 🌶🌶🌶 (HOT)

INGREDIENTS:

For the Wings:

- 1.5 kg chicken wings, split into drumettes and flats
- 1 tbsp baking powder (for extra crispiness)
- 1 tsp salt
- 1/2 cup (115g) unsalted butter
- 1/2 cup Frank's RedHot Original Cayenne Pepper Sauce
- 1 tbsp white vinegar
- 1/2 tsp garlic powder

For the Blue Cheese Dip:

- 1/2 cup sour cream
- 1/2 cup mayonnaise
- 1 cup crumbled blue cheese
- 1 tbsp lemon juice
- 1 tbsp fresh chives, chopped
- 2 tbsp milk (to thin, if needed)
- Salt and pepper to taste

METHOD:

1. For the Wings: Preheat oven to 120°C / 250°F. Place a wire rack on a baking sheet.
2. Pat the chicken wings completely dry with paper towels. In a large bowl, toss the wings with baking powder and salt until evenly coated.
3. Arrange the wings on the wire rack in a single layer. Bake for 30 minutes (this helps render the fat and dry the skin).
4. Increase oven temperature to 220°C / 425°F. Bake for another 40-50 minutes, turning halfway, until the wings are golden brown and very crispy.
5. For the Sauce: While the wings bake, melt the butter in a saucepan. Whisk in the hot sauce, vinegar, and garlic powder. Keep warm.
6. For the Dip: In a medium bowl, mash half of the blue cheese with a fork. Stir in the sour cream, mayonnaise, lemon juice, and chives. Fold in the remaining blue cheese. Add milk to reach your desired consistency. Season with salt and pepper.
7. When the wings are done, toss them thoroughly in the Buffalo sauce until glazed. Serve immediately with the blue cheese dip and celery sticks.

Two Secret Pro Tips (So You Don't End Up Like Trevor)

1. **Double Fry for Crunch:** Don't settle for limp wings. Fry them once to cook, let them rest, then fry again to get that shatter-level skin. You want that skin crisp enough to hear your ancestors whisper "good job."
2. **Toss, Don't Soak:** Wings should be coated, not drowning. A glossy sauce cling is the goal. Think golden retriever after a bath, not toddler in a mud pit.

Jalapeño Everything: The Green Bullet That Shot Through America's Soul

There's a special place in heaven, or probably a roadside diner off Route 66, for the first person who decided, "Hey, what if we just put jalapeños on... everything?" That person deserves a medal. Or at the very least, a lifetime supply of antacids and applause.

Before we unwrap the crispy, melty, bite-sized jalapeño magic that has infested everything from burgers to brownies (yes, really), let's do a quick headcount from where we just came. We survived Buffalo wings without burning off our taste buds, cooled them down with blue cheese like culinary firefighters, and lived to tell the tale. And now? It's time to meet the green chilli that thinks it's Beyoncé, always center stage, impossible to ignore, and somehow makes everything around it taste better.

From Sidekick to Superstar

Jalapeños used to be humble. A garnish. A little kick on the side. You know, like the parsley no one eats. But one day, someone deep-fried it, stuffed it with cheese, and suddenly this chilli was VIP, Very Important Pepper.

Let's be honest, you've seen jalapeños in more places than your cousin's Tinder profile. Nachos. Burgers. Hotdogs. Mac & cheese. Ice cream (no, I don't approve, but it exists). Somewhere in Wisconsin, there's a guy eating jalapeño-studded bratwurst while his wife nods approvingly in flannel. It's America's favorite edible daredevil.

And why not? Jalapeños are approachable heat. They don't scream like habaneros. They purr. A little bite, a lot of flavor. They're spicy without trying too hard, like the guy who plays acoustic guitar at parties and somehow gets away with it.

Jalapeño Poppers: The People's Crunch

Now let me tell you about poppers. Those cheeky little devils stuffed with cream cheese, wrapped in bacon, and deep-fried till they flirt with your arteries. I once brought a tray of these to a church potluck, and let's just say Sister Martha, aged 82, took three, winked at me, and said, "These are sinful, and I'm having another."

Moral of the story? If your food can make a nun blush, you're doing something right.

Want to impress a date, a football crowd, or your cat? Jalapeño poppers. They're crowd-pleasers, emotional support snacks, and mood lifters. You can bake 'em, grill 'em, or air-fry 'em if you're pretending to be healthy. But no matter how you make them, you'll always need more.

Green Rings of Power

Sliced jalapeños, pickled or fresh, are the green rings of power. Put them on a burger and boom, it's gourmet. Add them to eggs and you suddenly feel like a five-star hotel chef. Toss them on pizza and even the pineapple can't complain.

And can we talk about jalapeño cornbread? I mean, regular cornbread is already Grandma-level comforting. But jalapeños? They crash the party with their boots on. It's sweet. It's spicy. It's soft. It's bossy. It's a hug from someone who always speaks their mind.

Now, I know some folks are afraid of the heat. That's why I tell them this: jalapeños are not your enemy. They're your flavor therapist. They're not here to hurt you. They're here to make your cheese taste braver and your salsa sassier.

JALAPEÑO CORNBREAD

THE ULTIMATE COMFORT SIDE, NOW WITH A BIT OF SASS

YIELD: SERVES 8-10 **HEAT LEVEL: (MILD)**

INGREDIENTS:

- 1 cup cornmeal
- 1 cup plain flour
- 1/4 cup sugar
- 1 tbsp baking powder
- 1 tsp salt
- 1 cup milk
- 1 large egg
- 1/4 cup vegetable oil or melted butter
- 1 cup canned creamed corn
- 1-2 jalapeños, finely diced (seeds removed for less heat)
- 1 cup shredded cheddar cheese

METHOD:

1. Preheat oven to 200°C (400°F). Grease a 20cm (8-inch) square baking dish.
2. In a large bowl, whisk together the cornmeal, flour, sugar, baking powder, and salt.
3. In another bowl, whisk together the milk, egg, and oil. Pour the wet ingredients into the dry ingredients and stir until just combined. Do not overmix.
4. Fold in the creamed corn, diced jalapeños, and cheddar cheese.
5. Pour the batter into the prepared dish and bake for 20-25 minutes, or until a toothpick inserted into the centre comes out clean.
6. Let it cool for 10 minutes before slicing and serving

A Note from My Kitchen Catastrophe

One day, I got cocky. Decided to slice jalapeños without gloves, then casually rubbed my eye. Friends, it felt like my ancestors were slapping me with burning scrolls of regret. I screamed. I howled. I offered sacrifices to the dairy gods. Let this be your cautionary tale: always use gloves. Or a spoon. Or a psychic barrier.

Jalapeños in Dessert? Yep, That's Real Life.

Some folks have gone rogue and added jalapeños to brownies, cupcakes, and even cocktails. If you're brave, or reckless, go ahead. I tried a jalapeño-lime margarita once. It was like getting kissed and slapped at the same time.

Confusing, but oddly satisfying.

Just remember: balance is everything. Jalapeños need partners. Fat, dairy, sugar, those are their besties. Put them together and you'll get flavor fireworks, not just a five-alarm fire.

Southern BBQ with a Side of Fire

When it comes to BBQ, Americans don't whisper, they holler. They don't just grill, they glorify. It's a smoky, saucy, ritualistic performance of meat, fire, and pride that borders on religious zeal. But in the Southern states? They take it even further. This isn't just about slapping sauce on ribs. It's about generational secrets, homemade spice blends guarded like buried treasure, and a spice kick so bold it could make your grandpa cry into his cornbread.

Before we get into the meat sweats, let's check our seasoning: we've tangoed with Tex-Mex chilli con carne, dared to dip our fingers into Blue Cheese Rivers after tangy Buffalo wings, and dared jalapeños to do their worst. Now, we enter sacred territory, Southern BBQ, where flavour meets flame, and tradition takes the wheel.

Let me tell you a quick story.

There's a guy named Marvin. North Carolina born and bred, beard like a possum's tail and hands that smell like hickory smoke no matter how many times he washes. Marvin doesn't speak much. But give him a rack of ribs, and suddenly he's Maya Angelou with a basting brush. I met him at a cookout in Raleigh, where a single bite of his brisket almost made me propose marriage on the spot.

"What's the secret?" I asked, licking my fingers like a savage.
Marvin smiled, wiped his hands on a towel older than me, and said, "You season like you've got a point to prove."

Now that, my friend, is the Southern way. Spice isn't added for the sake of it, it's declaration, an accent in powdered form, a legacy poured from a shaker.

Southern BBQ rubs often include cayenne, paprika, crushed red pepper flakes, and chilli powder. But it's not just about heat. It's the harmony of sweet, smoky, tangy, and spicy that makes your tastebuds throw a block party in your mouth.

There are regional variations, of course. In Texas, they lean toward dry rubs and smoky slow-cooked brisket. In Memphis, it's all about ribs, sometimes dry, sometimes wet, and always delicious. Alabama throws in a curveball with their white BBQ sauce (made from mayo and vinegar), while Louisiana adds Cajun fire that'll make your eyelashes sweat.

One of my personal tricks? Add just a hint of chipotle in adobo to your BBQ sauce. That smoky-sweet burn hits different. It's the kind of heat that doesn't shout, but it leaves a voicemail you'll never forget.
Want another zinger? Try brushing a little peach jam mixed with cayenne on pork belly during the last ten minutes of grilling. Your guests won't know whether to weep or write you into their will.

And for the vegetarians thinking they're safe back there on the patio? Not so fast. Grilled jackfruit slathered in a spicy bourbon-BBQ sauce can hold its own against pulled pork, no questions asked. Add some smoked paprika, hot mustard, and crushed chipotle, and trust me, they'll be licking their palms clean.

Even cornbread isn't exempt. Try folding finely chopped jalapeños or green chillies into the batter, or serving it with a honey-chilli butter that slaps harder than a southern mama with a slipper.
At the heart of it, Southern BBQ isn't just about meat. It's about memory. It's about sweat on your brow, spice on your lips, and music in the background while someone's grandma judges your potato salad. It's family, it's fire, and it's fierce flavour.

So the next time you fire up the grill, don't just reach for salt and pepper. Reach for your heritage. Reach for boldness. Reach for that Marvin-level of soul-seasoning that says, "I didn't just cook this. I conquered it."
Because BBQ, dear reader, isn't just a meal. It's a statement.

13 SOUTH AMERICAN FIRE & FLAVOUR

As Mark Twain once said, "Part of the secret of success in life is to eat what you like and let the food fight it out inside." Well, welcome to South America, where the food doesn't just fight, it samba-kicks, salsa-twirls, and sucker-punches your taste buds with wild abandon.

If you thought you'd recovered from the Texan brisket and jalapeño hangover in the last chapter, bless your optimistic little soul. South America's not here to politely knock. It's kicking down the kitchen door with a basket full of chillies and a dance beat that won't quit.

We're about to journey from Peru's bright, citrus-splashed ceviches to Brazil's sultry, smoky feijoada, then tango through Argentina's chimichurri heat, and wrap it up with Chile's criminally underrated spicy gems. It's a whirlwind of heat, heart, and homemade sauces that'll make you shout, "¡Otra vez!" before your tongue cools off.

If Asia was a bold spice market carnival, South America is a spicy street dance with garlic, lime, and sweat on the rim of a cold beer glass.

Buckle up. No bland bites allowed in this chapter.

Peru – Aji Amarillo & Ceviche

There's a colour somewhere between mango sunset and defiant optimism. That colour is *aji amarillo*, and in Peru, it doesn't just show up on your plate, it performs.

Aji amarillo is the Zendaya of Peruvian chillies. Not too hot, not too shy—just the right amount of sass to command the spotlight without hijacking the stage."

Locals will tell you that if you haven't tasted this yellow beauty in a ceviche, you haven't really been to Peru. You've just loitered at the airport with a sad bag of peanuts.

Let's talk about ceviche. It's not just raw fish with attitude. It's a centuries-old culinary flex, a marinade so bold it "cooks" the fish without heat. Picture this: fresh chunks of sea bass bathed in lime juice, tossed with red onion slivers, *aji amarillo* paste, coriander, and sweet potato on the side. That's not lunch. That's smoky blues on a plate—slow, rich, and lingering like a note that refuses to end."

I once watched a Peruvian chef prepare ceviche on a beach in Miraflores. He moved with the confidence of a man who knew that every squeeze of lime could make or break reputations. He didn't measure. He didn't explain. He commanded. And when I tasted the result, my tongue stood up and saluted. The magic? It was all in the balance. The *aji amarillo* brought heat, sure, but it was a smiling heat, like a mischievous aunt pinching your cheek while handing you money. It didn't aim to destroy. It aimed to awaken.

Now, don't get carried away and toss any yellow chilli into the mix and call it "fusion." Respect the pepper. *Aji amarillo* is *Capsicum baccatum*, and it's been grown in Peru for over 7,000 years. It's fruity, slightly smoky, and has a Scoville rating around 30,000–50,000. That's spicy enough to flirt with danger, but not enough to require therapy.

PERUVIAN-STYLE CEVICHE WITH AJI AMARILLO

BRIGHT, CITRUSY, AND VIBRANT WITH A WARM, FRUITY HEAT.

YIELD: SERVES 4 AS AN APPETIZER **HEAT LEVEL:** 🌶🌶 (Medium)

INGREDIENTS:

- 500g fresh, firm white fish (e.g., sea bass, snapper, halibut), skinless, cut into 2cm cubes
- 1 red onion, very thinly sliced
- 1 cup fresh lime juice (about 10-12 limes)
- 2 tbsp aji amarillo paste
- 1 tbsp fresh ginger, grated
- 1 clove garlic, minced
- Salt to taste
- To serve: boiled sweet potato, boiled corn on the cob, fresh coriander leaves, lettuce cups

METHOD:

1. Place the sliced red onion in a bowl of ice water for 10 minutes to crisp and reduce its sharpness. Drain well.
2. In a large glass or ceramic bowl, whisk together the lime juice, aji amarillo paste, ginger, garlic, and salt.
3. Add the fish and the drained red onion to the lime juice mixture, ensuring the fish is completely submerged.
4. Let it marinate for 10-15 minutes, stirring gently once or twice. The fish will turn opaque as it "cooks" in the acid.
5. Serve immediately in bowls or on lettuce cups, accompanied by slices of sweet potato and corn on the cob. Garnish with coriander leaves

Pairing tip: *Aji amarillo* ceviche is brilliant with an icy Pisco Sour or chilled *chicha morada* (a sweet drink made from purple corn). One cools the fire. The other fans it. Your call.

Home cook alert: If you're outside Peru, look for frozen *aji amarillo* paste in Latin food stores. Don't substitute with random habanero and hope for the best. That's like playing Despacito at a tango party. Wrong vibe. Wrong continent.

Brazil – Spicy Feijoada & Sauces

Let me paint you a scene.

You walk into a Brazilian kitchen on a Saturday afternoon. The smell hits you first, deep, earthy, and bold. Somewhere between a grandma's hug and a back-alley drum circle. There's black beans bubbling in a pot so large it could double as a bathtub. Pork ribs swimming in it like they're on a vacation. Sausage slices gossiping with bay leaves. And then… there's the secret guest: *malagueta* pepper.

Now, feijoada isn't just a dish. It's an institution. It's the national meal of Brazil, and if you eat it wrong, too fast, too cold, too sober, your ancestors might whisper disapproval from beyond the grave.
But here's the twist: feijoada, traditionally, isn't face-meltingly hot. It's rich. It's smoky. It's comfort. The kind of food you eat slowly while someone tells a story about their cousin's cousin who once danced with a football star in Rio.

Yet, in Brazil's culinary underground (read: aunties who don't follow rules), a rogue pepper always finds its way in. Enter the *malagueta*. Small, shiny, and cocky. Don't be fooled by its size, it packs a Scoville punch of 60,000 to 100,000 units. That's enough to clear sinuses, secrets, and emotional baggage. Here's how the pros do it: they make a little side sauce called *molho de pimenta*. It's a wild blend of vinegar, garlic, oil, and sliced *malagueta* peppers. It sits on the table like a dare. Add a few drops to your feijoada and suddenly, the jazz band in your mouth goes from Bossa Nova to death metal, with rhythm.

Now, I tried this sauce in Bahia once. Big mistake. I poured it like ketchup. The chef didn't stop me. He watched. Smiled. Said, "*boa sorte.*" (Good luck.) Ten seconds later, I was sweating like a sinner in church, hiccuping like a broken engine. But strangely, I liked it.

That's the thing with Brazilian spice, it doesn't just hurt. It seduces. It teases. It comes in small doses that build like a samba beat. One-two-three, burn. One-two-three, bliss.

You can also spot this spicy spirit in Brazil's lesser-known chilli blends like *pimenta-de-cheiro*, more aromatic than fiery, and *dedo-de-moça* (literally "lady's finger"), a medium-heat beauty often pickled and served with meats. These chillies aren't just ingredients, they're personalities. They sass up your beans. They flirt with your rice.

And the sauces? Oh boy. Brazil has chilli-infused vinegars, chilli oils, and fermented pastes passed down like love letters between generations. Each household swears their version is best. And they're all right.

BRAZILIAN HOT SAUCE (MOLHO DE PIMENTA)

A SIMPLE, FIERY TABLE SAUCE TO AWAKEN ANY DISH

YIELD: MAKES ABOUT 1 CUP **HEAT LEVEL: 🌶🌶🌶 (HOT)**

INGREDIENTS:

- 1 cup malagueta peppers (or other small, hot red chillies), stems removed
- 3/4 cup white vinegar
- 2 cloves garlic
- 1/2 tsp salt
- 2 tbsp neutral oil (e.g., canola)

METHOD:

1. Combine the chillies, vinegar, garlic, and salt in a blender.
2. Blend until a coarse texture is achieved.
3. With the blender running, slowly drizzle in the oil to emulsify slightly.
4. Transfer to a sterilised glass jar. Let it sit for at least a day before using to allow the flavours to develop.

Pair it like a local: Feijoada and *malagueta* sauce are best balanced with *farofa* (toasted cassava flour), orange slices, collard greens, and if you're brave, a caipirinha. That's Brazil's national cocktail, lime, sugar, cachaça, and the reckless courage to dance after three glasses.

Home-cook heads-up: You can find *malagueta* in jars at most Latin or African grocery stores. But treat it with respect. Think of it as hot sauce's knife-wielding cousin, charming but not to be messed with.

Argentina – Chimichurri with a Kick

"Part steakhouse, part poetry slam, all spice."

That's how I once described Argentina to a friend who thought spice only belonged in tacos and Tinder bios.
See, Argentina's love affair with beef is no secret. It's legendary. Cows practically outnumber people. A proper *asado* (Argentine BBQ) isn't just a meal, it's a performance. The grill master, or *asador*, is the main act. The meat? The stage. And the audience? Well, if you don't applaud with your mouth full and sauce running down your chin, are you even Argentine?
But what gives these smoky, perfectly charred cuts of meat their final mic drop?

Chimichurri.

Now let me tell you, chimichurri isn't your average sauce. It's not shy, it's not sweet, and it doesn't care about fitting in. It's herbaceous, garlicky, acidic, and unapologetically bold. Like your friend who shows up overdressed to brunch and orders tequila at 10am.

Traditionally made with parsley, garlic, oregano, vinegar, olive oil, and red pepper flakes, chimichurri is the zesty, green crown sitting atop every proud slab of Argentine beef. Some families keep the heat tame. Others? They unleash the red chilli flakes like it's a fire sale.

There's even a red version, *chimichurri rojo* that swaps parsley for paprika and ups the chilli game like a DJ cranking the bass. Add in some crushed dried *ají molido* (a local crushed red pepper) and suddenly your medium-rare steak starts whispering, "You can't handle me."

But let's not ignore the real MVP here: the Argentine chilli scene is subtle but strategic. While Argentina isn't known for nuclear-level spice like its Andean cousins, it doesn't mean their sauces don't bite. They just sneak up on you. Like tango dancers. Smooth at first, then toe-stomping intense.

Take the *ají putaparió*, yes, it loosely translates to "go to hell." It's a fiery concoction made with chillies soaked in vinegar and sometimes paired with garlic and onion. Locals drizzle it on empanadas and *choripán* (that heavenly chorizo sandwich) like it's no big deal. You try it, and five seconds later your ears are sweating.

Now here's the deal: if you're making chimichurri at home, you have two choices, keep it classy or bring the heat. For beginners, I suggest a half-teaspoon of red pepper flakes. For thrill-seekers? Go wild. Toss in fresh chopped red chilli or a few drops of chilli oil and call it Chimichurri Diablo. Just don't blame me when your guests chug the table wine like it's holy water.

And speaking of wine, Malbec is your partner in this culinary crime. It balances the vinegar bite, cools the heat, and makes everything taste like you've just been kissed by a sultry stranger under a Buenos Aires moon.

CLASSIC CHIMICHURRI SAUCE

THE VIBRANT, HERBY SAUCE THAT MAKES ANY GRILLED MEAT SING

YIELD: MAKES ABOUT 1 CUP **HEAT LEVEL: 🌶🌶 (MEDIUM)**

INGREDIENTS:

- 1 cup fresh flat-leaf parsley, finely chopped
- 3-4 cloves garlic, minced
- 2 tbsp fresh oregano, finely chopped (or 2 tsp dried)
- 1 shallot or 1/2 small red onion, finely chopped
- 1/2 cup extra virgin olive oil
- 2 tbsp red wine vinegar
- 1 tbsp lemon juice
- 1 tsp red pepper flakes (or 1 fresh red chilli, finely chopped)
- 3/4 tsp sea salt
- 1/2 tsp freshly ground black pepper

METHOD:

1. Combine the chopped parsley, garlic, oregano, and shallot in a medium bowl.

2. Stir in the olive oil, red wine vinegar, and lemon juice.

3. Season with red pepper flakes, salt, and black pepper. Stir to combine.

4. Let the sauce sit for at least 30 minutes at room temperature to allow the flavours to meld before serving. Store leftovers in the fridge for up to a week.

From fire-kissed beef to herb-laced heat, Argentina knows how to whisper spice through flavour, not flames.

But don't hang up your sombrero yet, we're heading to Chile next, where the heat doesn't come screaming... it simmers with quiet confidence. Ready for that quiet assassin? Let's go.

Chile – The Unsung Heat Hero

If Argentina is that friend who charms the crowd with a flamboyant grill and a shot of Malbec, then Chile is the quiet genius at the corner of the party, reserved, refined, but packing heat you never saw coming.

Let's just say this: Chile is not loud about its chillies, but oh, they work in silence like a kettle about to scream.

You see, most people associate South American spice with Peru's flamboyant *aji amarillo* or Brazil's fiery *malagueta*. Chile, on the other hand, often slips under the radar. Maybe it's because the country's known more for wine, mountains, and moody poets like Pablo Neruda. But what many overlook is that Chile is sitting on a goldmine of flavour bombs, tucked in clay pots, backyard grills, and little jars your *abuela* guards like national secrets.

Let's start with the humble *ají cristal*. Pale yellow, crunchy, and deceptively mellow at first bite, this pepper lulls you into a false sense of friendship. But give it a minute. It's like a Chilean telenovela, starts soft, ends in betrayal and tears. When roasted and blended into *pebre*, a salsa-like condiment of coriander, garlic, and olive oil, it's absolute sorcery. Locals will casually smear it on bread like it's nothing, and you'll be sitting there googling "why is my tongue crying?"

Or take the *rocoto*. While not exclusive to Chile, its southern variants are packed into seafood stews and marinated dishes that tease your senses like a dangerous flirt. I once watched a local fisherman in Valparaíso lace a bowl of *caldillo de congrio* (fish soup) with *rocoto*, wink at me, and say, "Just enough to keep your heart beating." Honestly, it nearly stopped mine.

Then there's the *ají cacho de cabra*, goat's horn chilli. Now this one? She doesn't play. Long, red, and slightly wrinkled like a retired matador, this dried beauty is the backbone of *chancho en piedra*, a kind of volcanic mortar-smashed salsa that's as rustic as it sounds. The smokiness and the slow heat burn are perfect for those who like their fire like they like their drama, slow, creeping, and unforgettable (Muñoz, 2020).

But why does Chile's chilli game get so little global airtime?

Blame the branding. The country's spice culture is woven into everyday dishes, not sold as spectacle. It's a quiet tradition, not a TikTok trend. You won't see Chilean grandmas filming "Death by Chilli Challenge" videos.

You'll find them making *porotos granados* (bean stew) with *ají* that builds heat like a whispered secret (Zamora, 2017).

And the geography? Oh, that's the sauce. Chile's ridiculously long terrain, from the bone-dry Atacama in the north to the rainy fjords of Patagonia, creates diverse growing zones that birth a rainbow of chillies with unique characters. It's like nature's spicy mixtape, curated by volcanoes, sea breezes, and pure culinary sorcery (Valdés & Riquelme, 2019).

Now, if you're feeling brave and want to channel some Chilean fire into your kitchen, start with a *chancho en piedra*. You'll need ripe tomatoes, garlic, a mortar and pestle, olive oil, and of course, dried *ají cacho de cabra*. Rehydrate that chilli in warm water, mash it like you're angry, and mix everything until it becomes a thick, deep red paste of sin.

Spread it on toast, grilled meats, or even drizzle it over roasted veggies. One bite and you'll understand why Chilean heat doesn't knock, it tiptoes in and rearranges your entire idea of flavour.

PEBRE (CHILEAN FRESH SALSA)

THE EVERYDAY CHILEAN TABLE SAUCE THAT'S FRESH, ZINGY, AND SPICY

YIELD: MAKES ABOUT 1.5 CUPS **HEAT LEVEL:)) (MEDIUM)**

INGREDIENTS:

- 2 medium tomatoes, finely diced
- 1/2 cup red onion, finely diced
- 1-2 ají cristal or other medium-hot green chillies, finely chopped
- 2 cloves garlic, minced
- 1/2 cup fresh coriander, chopped
- 1/3 cup olive oil
- 3 tbsp red wine vinegar
- Salt to taste

METHOD:

1. Combine the diced tomatoes, onion, chillies, garlic, and coriander in a bowl.
2. Whisk together the olive oil and red wine vinegar. Pour over the tomato mixture and toss to combine.
3. Season generously with salt. Let it sit for at least 30 minutes before serving to allow the flavours to meld. Serve with bread, on grilled meats, or as a condiment for beans.

So, there you have it, Chile, the silent spice sniper of South America.

14 CHILLI-LACED DRINKS & COCKTAILS

"Too much of anything is bad, but too much good whiskey is barely enough.", Mark Twain.

I don't know if Twain ever tried a jalapeño margarita, but if he had, he might've added a dash of hot sauce to that quote.

Welcome to the cocktail chapter, the naughty corner of our chilli party. You've chewed your way through global firestorms, danced with Peruvian aji, flirted with Vietnamese bird's eye, and given Tex-Mex your undivided attention. Now, it's time to drink the flame.

This chapter isn't about getting tipsy; it's about teasing your tastebuds with the kind of drinks that whisper, "I'm sweet," then slap you mid-sip. It's for the brave, the curious, and the cocktail heretics who think cucumbers are boring unless they're booby-trapped with chilli.

Whether you're the hostess with the mostest or someone who just wants to feel sophisticated while secretly crying into a spicy Bloody Mary, we've got something to wet your palate and wake up your sinuses.

From margaritas that flirt to cucumber coolers with bite, each section here will raise your glass, and your eyebrows.

Chilli Vodka, Tequila & Infusions: Bottled Mischief with a Kick

Here's the thing about chilli-infused booze: it's like inviting a mischievous cousin to your quiet dinner party. At first, they smile sweetly. Then they spike the punch and teach grandma how to salsa.

If you thought Margaritas were wild, buckle your seatbelt, because chilli-infused vodka and tequila don't knock politely. They kick the door in, wearing glitter boots and holding a jalapeño hostage.

Infusing 101: It's Not Just a Pinterest Hobby

Let's demystify the magic. Infusing alcohol is essentially letting booze and flavour fall madly in love. It's you, playing Cupid with a chilli and a bottle of tequila.

The basics:

- **Pick your weapon:** Vodka, tequila, or even mezcal for the bold.
- **Choose your chilli:** Jalapeños are a safe bet. Habaneros? Only if you've written your will.
- **Slice, drop, wait.** Taste after 24 hours. Taste again. Then remove the chillies before it tastes like a tequila exorcism.

Fun fact: The Scoville scale doesn't lose potency in alcohol. If anything, it intensifies as capsaicin binds to ethanol molecules (Lopez et al., 2017).

One time, I left a bird's eye chilli in vodka for three days. Rookie mistake. That shot burned so bad it sobered up my entire ancestry.

Vodka's Secret Life as a Spice Canvas

Vodka is the introvert of spirits—quiet, neutral, always agreeable. But add chilli? It becomes a pyromaniac with a PhD in fun. A single chilli can add depth, heat, and a lingering kick to an otherwise forgettable sip (Gupta, 2019).

Use it in:

- Bloody Marys with backbone.
- A Martini with a plot twist.
- A simple vodka tonic with a whisper of fire.

Pair with cucumber or lime to balance the drama. Because even divas need stage managers.

Tequila Gets Its Groove Back

Now let's talk tequila, your emotionally unpredictable ex. One moment it's smooth and citrusy, the next it's got you doing karaoke in a sombrero. When infused with chillies, tequila becomes a high-voltage dance partner. It demands your attention and doesn't apologise for the bruises.

Infuse it with:

- Jalapeño and mango slices for tropical chaos.

- Habanero and pineapple for masochistic delight.
- Chipotle for a smoky, cowboy-winking finish.

Bartenders call this technique “aggressive layering,” and it’s rising in craft cocktail circles globally (Peterson, 2022).

A friend once served habanero-infused tequila at a house party. Someone tried it, coughed dramatically, and declared, “I’ve just tasted hell, and I liked it.”

Safety First, Party Second

Before you get wild, a word of caution. Chilli-infused alcohol should never feel like punishment. Test in small batches. Gloves are your friend when chopping chillies. And warn your guests. Nothing ruins a night faster than someone accidentally drinking lava.

Unless you’re trying to settle old scores. Then by all means, hand them a shot glass and smile.

Non-Alcoholic Zing: Iced Teas & Cucumber Coolers

A few years ago, I met a woman at a backyard BBQ who brought a "detox" cucumber water and left with a spicy ginger-mint tea in one hand and a bag of ribs in the other. That, my friend, is the power of a good non-alcoholic chilli drink—it doesn’t whisper “wellness.” It smirks and says, “I came for the kick.”

After a whole book’s worth of fire-kissed meats, sweets, and smoky sauces, it’s time to hydrate like a legend without sacrificing flavour. And let’s be honest, not every guest wants to guzzle tequila. Some want a clean conscience with a slap of zing. So, what do we give them? Drinks that flirt with spice but still keep their halo. Think iced teas, citrusy infusions, cool cucumber medleys, and even chilli-touched lemonades.

GINGER-CHILLI ICED TEA

THE THROAT HUG WITH ATTITUDE

YIELD: SERVES 6 **HEAT LEVEL: 🌶🌶 (MEDIUM)**

INGREDIENTS:

- 1 litre strong-brewed black tea, cooled
- 3-inch piece of fresh ginger, grated
- 1 red chilli, thinly sliced (seeds in for more heat)
- Juice of 1 lemon
- Honey or agave to taste
- Lemon wheels and crushed ice, to serve

METHOD:

1. Combine the cooled tea, grated ginger, sliced chilli, and lemon juice in a large pitcher.
2. Sweeten with honey or agave to your liking.
3. Refrigerate for at least 2 hours to let the flavours infuse.
4. Serve over crushed ice, garnished with a lemon wheel.

CUCUMBER CHILLI COOLER (SPA WATER WITH A REVENGE PLOT)

AS REFRESHING AS SKINNY-DIPPING AT MIDNIGHT.

YIELD: SERVES 4 **HEAT LEVEL: 🌶 (MILD)**

INGREDIENTS:

- 1 litre sparkling water
- 1 cucumber, thinly sliced
- 1 lime, thinly sliced
- 1 jalapeño or bird's eye chilli, thinly sliced
- Pinch of sea salt
- Handful of fresh mint leaves

METHOD:

1. Combine all ingredients in a large pitcher.
2. Let it sit in the fridge for at least an hour for the flavours to meld.
3. Serve chilled, and watch as it bites just enough to remind you you're alive.

PINEAPPLE CHILLI SLUSH

TASTES LIKE A TROPICAL HOLIDAY... UNTIL THE FIRE CREEPS IN.

YIELD: SERVES 2

HEAT LEVEL: (MILD)

INGREDIENTS:

- 3 cups frozen pineapple chunks
- Juice of 1 lime
- 2 tablespoons honey
- A pinch of cayenne pepper
- Splash of water or coconut water to blend

METHOD:

1. Combine all ingredients in a high-speed blender.
2. Blend until thick and frosty.
3. Pour into glasses and serve immediately.

A good drink isn't just wet. It tells a story. It has plot twists. Your first sip says "cool and citrusy," and just as you exhale, boom, the chilli hits. Not harsh. Just enough to say, "Don't underestimate me."

If you're hosting a party and want to serve something gorgeous, go for a Chilli-Basil Lemonade Pitcher. Lemons, basil leaves, a touch of agave, and crushed red chilli flakes stirred into filtered water. Serve it in mason jars with lemon wheels and a rim of pink salt. Guests will ask for the recipe. You'll pretend it was passed down from your great-aunt in Oaxaca. I won't tell.

Dessert Cocktails with Heat

They say revenge is best served cold. But I say, dessert is best served with heat—specifically, the kind that tickles your throat, makes your eyebrows dance, and pairs perfectly with chocolate, cream, or a cheeky night in.

First, let's take a breath and honour the path we've walked. We've zested lemons, roasted jalapeños, turned cucumbers into bold beverages and pineapple into tropical fireworks. And now, we arrive at the grand finale. The spicy encore. The curtain call that says, "Yes, darling, I came here to burn and be fabulous."

THE SPICY CHOCOLATE MARTINI

DESSERT PUT ON STILETTOS AND STARTED WHISPERING NAUGHTY SECRETS

YIELD: SERVES 1

HEAT LEVEL: 🌶🌶 (MEDIUM)

INGREDIENTS:

- 60 ml chilli-infused vodka
- 30 ml dark chocolate liqueur
- 15 ml fresh cream or full-fat coconut milk
- 1 teaspoon dark chocolate syrup
- A dash of ancho chilli powder
- Ice

METHOD:

1. Fill a cocktail shaker with ice.
2. Add all the liquid ingredients.
3. Shake vigorously until well-chilled.
4. Strain into a chilled martini glass.
5. Garnish with a light dusting of ancho chilli powder.

CHILLI-SPIKED ESPRESSO CREAM LIQUEUR

CRUNCHY, CREAMY, AND SWEET WITH A FIERY FINISH.

YIELD: MAKES ABOUT 500 ML **HEAT LEVEL: 🌶 (MILD)**

INGREDIENTS:

- 250 ml strong espresso, cooled
- 200 ml sweetened condensed milk
- 100 ml cream
- 1 teaspoon vanilla extract
- 1 small red chilli, sliced in half (remove for less heat)

METHOD:

1. Combine all ingredients in a large jar or bottle.
2. Seal tightly and shake vigorously for one minute.
3. Refrigerate for at least 4 hours, or overnight, for the flavours to meld.
4. Remove the chilli slice before serving over ice.

COCONUT MANGO FIRETAIL

MAKES YOU FEEL LIKE YOU'RE ON A HAMMOCK IN RIO WHILE TRAINING FOR HOT ONES.

YIELD: SERVES 2 **HEAT LEVEL: (MILD)**

INGREDIENTS:

- 1 cup frozen mango chunks
- 1/2 cup coconut cream
- 60 ml white rum (optional)
- Juice of 1 lime
- A generous pinch of cayenne pepper
- Ice

METHOD:

1. Combine all ingredients in a blender.
2. Blend until smooth and creamy.
3. Pour into tall glasses and serve immediately

THE CHILLI CREAM BOMB (A SHOT)

A FIREWORK WRAPPED IN A FLUFFY CLOUD.

YIELD: SERVES 1 **HEAT LEVEL: 🌶🌶🌶 (HOT)**

INGREDIENTS:

- 250 ml strong espresso, cooled
- 200 ml sweetened condensed milk
- 100 ml cream
- 1 teaspoon vanilla extract
- 1 small red chilli, sliced in half (remove for less heat)

METHOD:

1. Carefully pour the chilli liqueur into a shot glass.
2. Gently layer the cold whipped cream on top.
3. Dust with cinnamon.
4. Instruct your guest to down it in one gulp for the full fire-and-ice effect.

Hosting Tip: Set up a "Burn or Bliss" mini bar. Let guests pick their own chilli level with colour-coded drink cards: Green for mild, Yellow for playful heat, and Red for "Call my mother, I saw God." It's fun, interactive, and saves you from repeating the phrase "it's not that spicy" seventeen times.

15 CHILLI FOR BRUNCH, LUNCH & LAZY DAYS

"A Sunday well spent brings a week of content." But what nobody tells you is that the secret sauce to a well-spent Sunday might just involve actual sauce, with chillies.

First of all, you've made it to Chapter 15. That's fifteen chapters of flavour, fire, and foolishly good fun. If you're still here, bless your resilient tongue. We've travelled across continents, spooned hot sauces into desserts, dunked jalapeños in margaritas, and survived Scotch bonnets without calling the fire department. You, my friend, are not just a reader; you're a chilli warrior.

Now we land in the land of lazy days. Those glorious in-between hours when nothing is urgent, everything tastes better, and your fridge is one good idea away from magic. Brunches that run into lunch. Lunches that morph into naps. Leftovers that become legend.

This chapter is where we tone down the ceremony but keep the flavour cranked. Think: soft eggs with a devilish drizzle, zesty slaws, leftover sauces rising like phoenixes, and 10-minute fixes that taste like an hour-long miracle. Comfort food, but with a chilli halo.

Ready? Because this is where chilli becomes your coziest, sassiest companion. Now let's start with the best way to ruin plain toast forever.

Spicy Egg Dishes & Toast Toppers

You know that moment when toast pops up from the toaster and just stares at you, bare, beige, and begging for meaning? That's your cue to play God with a bottle of chilli oil and a dozen eggs. Because plain toast is just edible cardboard until you slap on some heat and glory.

Let's talk eggs. Scrambled, fried, poached, or boiled, eggs are like that chill friend who can hang with anyone but secretly thrives on drama. And chilli is the drama. Whether it's a smear of gochujang under your yolk, a swirl of sriracha in your scramble, or a confetti of red pepper flakes over your sunny-side-up, chilli lifts eggs from "meh" to "marry me."

One morning, I whipped up a Turkish-style menemen (soft eggs with peppers and tomatoes) and added a sneaky spoon of harissa. My neighbour, who only came over to borrow sugar, ended up sitting down and asking for a second plate. That's the chilli effect. It doesn't knock. It kicks the door in and brings a party.

Now let's not forget toast. Oh, toast. Avocado toast may have had its Instagram moment, but chilli-fried eggs on toast? That's the flavour revolution nobody saw coming. Picture this: a thick sourdough slice, buttery and golden, with a soft-fried egg on top, then drizzled with homemade chilli crisp that sizzles as it hits the heat. The crunch. The runny yolk. The heat. It's less of a snack, more of a spiritual awakening.

Feeling posh? Whip up a quick chilli-lime hollandaise and pour it over poached eggs and toast. Or go rustic: add chopped green chillies to your scrambled eggs, toss in leftover herbs, and call it brunch with a vengeance.

And for the sweet rebels? Try chilli-honey butter on toast with scrambled eggs. Trust me, your mouth will be confused, but delighted.

Midday Heat: Salads & Slaws with Bite

Now, I know what you're thinking: Salads? With chilli? Isn't that like putting rollerblades on a snail? But hear me out. We're not talking about the limp lettuce sadness that shows up at office potlucks. We're talking power-packed, lip-tingling, nap-optional bowls of midday glory.

In the last section, we cracked eggs with spice and turned toast into spicy gold. But now it's time for something crisp, fresh, and just a little dangerous. Like a good gossip session over lunch—crunchy, juicy, a little heat, and very satisfying.

Let's start with slaws. These crunchy rebels are perfect blank canvases. Add red cabbage, carrots, and thinly sliced fennel, then toss in a dressing of lime juice, honey, and a whisper (okay, a loud whisper) of minced jalapeño. Suddenly, your fridge leftovers have entered their glow-up era.

Want to take it global? Add gochujang to a sesame vinaigrette for a Korean fusion slaw that'll make your weekday lunch feel like a K-drama plot twist (Kim & Lee, 2020). Or add roasted peanuts and bird's eye chilli to a papaya slaw for a Thai-style crunch that sings in five spicy octaves (Sritong et al., 2021).

And salads? They don't have to be dainty. Picture this: grilled corn, avocado, black beans, charred red pepper, and fresh coriander. Now finish it with a smoky chipotle-lime dressing and just watch your coworkers side-eye your lunchbox with jealous hunger.

Here's the trick: balance. If your salad is a rock band, chilli is the electric guitar. It doesn't need to scream the whole time, just rip the solo when it counts. Pair heat with fats (avocados, nuts, tahini) to round off the edges, and toss in some fruit (mango, pomegranate, pineapple) to hit that sweet-spicy high note (Mendoza, 2022).

One of my all-time favourites? Watermelon, feta, mint, and red chilli flakes. It sounds like a kitchen dare, but trust me, it's like your taste buds went on holiday to Ibiza.

So, if you've been treating salads like the background dancers of lunch, it's time to put them centre stage. Let the greens strut, the chillies sizzle, and your taste buds thank you in five languages.

Leftover Magic: Sauces Reimagined

Now, if the last section left you whispering sweet nothings to a jalapeño-laced coleslaw, buckle up, because we're about to romance your leftovers into something worthy of a second date.

Let me ask you a hard truth: how many times have you stared into your fridge like it's the Bermuda Triangle, hoping for dinner to assemble itself from last night's debris? We've all done the "I'll just reheat this rice and slap something on it" dance. But here's a secret: leftover sauces, especially spicy ones, are not leftovers. They're ingredients wearing yesterday's clothes, with the power to seduce today's meal.

Take chilli oil, for example. That glorious jar of red-gold fire from last night's stir-fry? Drizzle it over eggs, toss it into a mayo base for a smoky aioli, or swirl it into hummus for a scandalously spicy dip. It's like giving your condiment shelf a passport and saying, "Go be great." According to culinary expert Fuchsia Dunlop, "chilli oils and pastes improve with age, gaining complexity that can transform simple dishes" (Dunlop, 2006). I mean, who wouldn't want a condiment with the emotional depth of a Netflix drama?

And then there's leftover salsa. Not the sad, watery kind from the back of the fridge, but the chunky, garlicky masterpiece you made for taco night. Blend it into a vinaigrette. Simmer it down with a touch of stock for a soup base. Or stir it through pasta with some cheese and chopped coriander for an Italian-Mexican lovechild that'll confuse and delight your dinner guests. One study even found that integrating spicy condiments into routine meals can enhance satiety and reduce snacking, especially in the midday slump (Yoshioka et al., 2004).

Don't forget chutneys and sambals, those tangy, punchy little divas of the sauce world. Mix them into yogurt for a cooling but fiery dip, or combine with soy sauce and a dash of sesame oil for an instant dumpling drizzle. As *Bon Appétit* writer Priya Krishna puts it, "leftover chutneys are like edible jazz; you riff, and something unexpected (and delicious) happens" (Krishna, 2018).

The goal here isn't just food waste reduction (although your compost bin will weep tears of joy). It's flavour reimagination. It's turning "leftover" into "legendary." So open that fridge with swagger. Look those sauces in the eye and whisper, "You up?"

Heat in a Hurry: 10-Minute Fixes

You know those moments when hunger hits like a toddler on a sugar crash? There's no patience, no grace, just pure desperation. That's when the 10-minute chilli fix steps in like a culinary superhero in flip-flops. Whether you're hungover, late for a Zoom call, or just too lazy to pretend you know what quinoa is, these quick-fire chilli meals are the edible equivalent of a mic drop.

CHILLI GARLIC NOODLES

A FIERY BOWL THAT'LL MAKE YOUR TASTEBUDS DO THE ELECTRIC SLIDE.

YIELD: SERVES 1 **HEAT LEVEL: 🌶🌶 (MEDIUM)**

INGREDIENTS:

- 1 portion of pre-cooked noodles (ramen, udon, or rice noodles)
- 1 tbsp chilli oil
- 2 cloves garlic, minced
- 1 tbsp soy sauce
- Handful of leftover veggies (e.g., sliced bell peppers, spinach, spring onions)
- Optional: 1 soft-boiled egg, sesame seeds

METHOD:

1. Cook noodles according to package instructions. Drain.
2. While noodles are cooking, heat chilli oil in a pan over medium heat.
3. Add garlic and stir-fry for 30 seconds until fragrant.
4. Toss in your veggies and stir-fry for 1-2 minutes until slightly softened.
5. Add the cooked noodles and soy sauce. Toss everything together until well-coated and heated through.
6. Serve immediately, topped with a soft-boiled egg and sesame seeds if desired.

SPICY FRIED EGG WRAP

THE ULTIMATE LAZY-DAY SAVIOUR.

YIELD: SERVES 1 **HEAT LEVEL: 🌶 (MILD)**

INGREDIENTS:

- 1 large tortilla
- 1 egg
- Handful of grated cheese
- 1 tsp chopped fresh chilli or a squirt of sriracha
- Handful of baby spinach
- Salt and pepper

METHOD:

1. Place the tortilla in a non-stick pan over medium heat.

2. Crack the egg directly onto the tortilla and spread the white slightly.

3. Sprinkle with cheese, chilli, salt, and pepper.

4. Once the egg white begins to set, carefully flip the entire tortilla.

5. Cook for another minute until the egg is cooked to your liking and the tortilla is golden.

6. Remove from heat, scatter with spinach, fold, and devour

3-INGREDIENT CHILLI TUNA TOAST

YOU'LL THANK ME WHEN YOU'RE EATING THIS IN YOUR PJS AT 11:59 AM.

YIELD: SERVES 1 **HEAT LEVEL: 🌶 (MILD)**

INGREDIENTS:

- 1 can of tuna, drained
- 2 tbsp mayonnaise
- 1 tbsp chopped jalapeños (from a jar is fine!)
- 1 thick slice of bread, toasted

METHOD:

1. Preheat your grill.

2. Mix the tuna, mayo, and jalapeños in a bowl.

3. Pile the mixture onto the toast.

4. Grill for 2-3 minutes until bubbly and golden.

The beauty of these quick chilli fixes is that they don't ask for your resume or your best apron. They just show up, make you sweat a little, and leave you full and oddly proud. They're perfect for students, single dads, overworked humans, or anyone who has googled "how to cook without cooking."

You don't need to be a kitchen god to whip up heat in a hurry. You just need one thing: a stash of chilli condiments that don't require a PhD in fermentation. Keep sriracha, sambal oelek, hot sauce, or even a rogue chilli pickle jar around, and you're in business (Wang & Yang, 2021). Also, having pre-cut veggies and some form of carb—bread, rice, or noodles—makes this even more foolproof (Tang, 2018).

The real takeaway here? Speed and spice are not mutually exclusive. Just because it's fast doesn't mean it has to taste like a soggy napkin. Add chilli smartly, and you've got a five-star bite with a two-star effort.

16 ENTERTAINING WITH A GLOBAL HEAT MAP

If your dinner parties usually involve a bag of chips, a Spotify playlist on shuffle, and someone awkwardly asking, "So... what do you do?", then pull up a chair, friend, we're about to upgrade your social life with the fierce, fabulous force of global chilli power.

Hosting with heat isn't just about cooking something spicy and hoping nobody cries. It's about storytelling through spice. You're not serving a meal; you're serving a mini world tour. Each dish is a boarding pass. Each drink, a cheeky layover. And by the end of the night, if your guests aren't begging for a passport or at least another shot of chilli tequila, you're doing it wrong.

In the last chapter, we flirted with lazy-day brunches, quick-fix feasts, and leftover magic. Now, we're swapping solo stove time for group chaos—the good kind. Think chilli trivia over cocktails. Sambal tasting with soundtracks. Peri-peri with a side of costume drama.

In this chapter, we'll plan the ultimate spicy theme night, match chillies with music and culture, throw in some games that don't involve crying into hot sauce, and end with saucy decor ideas that'd make your aunty blush. Ready to host the hottest party on the block?

Planning Your Spicy Theme Night

Martha Stewart might know how to fold napkins into swans, but can she throw a chilli-themed fiesta that crosses continents and leaves guests sweating with joy? Probably not. But you? You're about to.

So, here's the game plan: You're not just throwing a dinner party; you're crafting an edible expedition. Your living room becomes an airport. Your guests? Hungry, wide-eyed travellers. And your dishes? Glorious, tongue-tingling destinations.

Let's start simple: Pick a heat level.

Like dating apps and rollercoasters, spice tolerance varies. You don't want to serve ghost pepper margaritas to someone who cries eating bell peppers. Set expectations early—maybe even include a cheeky "heat index" on your invite:

🌶 = Grandma can handle it
🌶🌶 = Bring water
🌶🌶🌶 = Sign this waiver

Next: Choose your chilli regions.

Are you going full Mexican cantina with sombreros and salsas? A fiery Indian curry corner with Bollywood beats? Or a pan-Asian inferno with Thai bird's eye bites and Gochujang-glazed wings?

Pro tip: Pick 2–3 countries and curate a few signature bites from each. Keeps it spicy without spiralling into kitchen chaos.

Now, set the vibe.

Music matters. You can't serve Brazilian feijoada in silence. Spotify has global party playlists that slap harder than wasabi on a paper cut. Think Reggaeton for Latin flair, Afrobeat for West African stews, K-Pop while slurping Korean fire noodles. Match the rhythm to the region.

Don't forget the dress code.

"Come as your spice level" is a hit. Mild = beige and polite. Medium = bold colors, maybe a printed scarf. Hot = flaming reds, feathers, possibly glitter. The braver the outfit, the braver the tastebuds (in theory).

Interactive elements? Yes, please.

Have a "Chilli Passport" station where guests stamp countries as they try different dishes. Award small prizes for "World's Sweatiest Forehead" or "Best Dramatic Reaction to Spice." Just no shaming; spice tolerance is not a moral compass.

And timing is everything.

Don't serve the spiciest dish first. That's like making someone run a marathon before teaching them to walk. Start with mild crowd-pleasers—jalapeño poppers, mango salsas—then escalate gradually until you hit the fire-breathing finale.

Also, have cool-down zones.

Milk-based drinks, cucumber slices, and Greek yogurt dips are your safety nets. Keep them visible, easy to access, and cheekily labeled like "Emergency Exit" or "Tongue Triage."

Here's one last golden tip: Ask your guests to bring something.
But not just any old thing. Challenge them: "Bring a dish or a drink inspired by your family's weirdest relationship with chilli." I once had a friend show up with peri-peri ice cream. Was it edible? Barely. Was it memorable? Absolutely.

And if you really want to level up, create a fiery photo wall.
Flaming emojis, passport stamps, a giant "Heat Level" meter guests can pose under. This isn't just about food; it's about memory-making. With spice.

Chilli & Culture Pairings: Mood, Music, Menu

They say music feeds the soul, but pair it with chilli and you've got a full-blown flavour fiesta where your tongue dances salsa while your hips follow suit. Welcome to the wild, steamy world of chilli and culture pairings, where mood meets menu, and music spices up more than just the background.

But first, let's talk about vibe alignment. Imagine walking into a Moroccan-themed dinner, candles flickering like belly dancer hips, and instead of the hypnotic thrum of a darbuka drum… you hear techno. That's like putting ketchup on a tajine—legally questionable.

Culture sets the table. Chilli sets the pace. Music ties it all together. And when you blend these elements just right, your party becomes a full sensory journey. Here's how I do it:

1. Mexico: Mariachi Heat
For a Mexican-themed gathering, we're talking mariachi magic, folk guitars, sombreros slightly askew, and a buffet that could make Frida Kahlo weep. Play tracks from Vicente Fernández while serving smoky chipotle tacos and habanero salsa that demands respect. Add a DIY margarita bar, and suddenly everyone thinks they can dance the Jarabe Tapatío, even if they just twisted an ankle trying.

2. India: Sitar Meets Sizzle
Let your playlist simmer with the sounds of Ravi Shankar and A.R. Rahman, then bring in tandoori heat and masala bites that kiss your tastebuds gently before setting them on fire. Indian gatherings are all about generosity—food piled like mini mountains, colours clashing joyfully, and enough cardamom to perfume the whole neighbourhood (Mann et al., 2020).

Pro tip: Serve smaller portions of various dishes, like chilli paneer skewers or pav bhaji sliders, so guests can sample their way through the subcontinent without entering a food coma.

3. Caribbean Carnival

Cue the soca beats, crack open the jerk seasoning, and blast the colour. The Caribbean isn't a theme; it's an experience, and Scotch bonnet is your MC. Pair grilled jerk chicken with plantain fritters, reggae and rum, and your guests will be whining like they've been possessed by the rhythm gods (Taylor, 2018).

Mood matters: Warm lighting, barefoot vibes, and maybe a dance contest after dinner to help guests "sweat out" the scotch bonnet regret.

4. Middle Eastern Mezze & Mild Heat

Middle Eastern spice is more about depth than danger. You want oud music humming in the background, slow-cooked lamb sprinkled with Aleppo pepper, and tables overflowing with harissa hummus, stuffed grape leaves, and pomegranate-drizzled magic. The heat here whispers, never shouts (El-Wakil, 2021).

This is your elegant soirée zone. Think floor cushions, candle-lit corners, and storytelling with mint tea. Chilli isn't about dominance here; it's about depth.

Matching music and mood to menu isn't just extra; it's essential if you want your spicy night to be remembered longer than your cousin's wedding. When chilli travels, it doesn't just bring flavour; it carries the heartbeat of entire cultures.

Games, Tastings & Challenges

"Life is too short for boring food, and even shorter if you challenge Nana to a ghost pepper dare."

If you thought chilli was just for stirring into sauces, think again. It's also the ultimate party starter, the real MVP of any evening that's threatening to become… well, beige. We're talking games, tastings, and challenges, where grown adults cry gracefully into milk and your cousin discovers the meaning of humility with a Scotch Bonnet.

So, pull on your brave pants, stock up on dairy, and let's turn your kitchen into a spicy colosseum.

1. The Heat Ladder Tasting Table

Let's start civilised before things spiral. Picture this: a table lined with labelled hot sauces, each one climbing up the Scoville ladder like it's training for the chilli Olympics. Guests take turns sampling from mild to wild, rating them on taste, heat, and emotional betrayal.

Add mini scorecards, give points for "best flavour," "sneaky spice," and "most likely to end a friendship." Include a few local favourites from your region and one wildcard from a country whose cuisine laughs in the face of subtlety (López-García, 2020).

2. Guess That Spice! Blindfold Edition
This one's part game, part sensory awakening, and part revenge for whoever last asked, "Is this spicy?" while holding a jalapeño.

Blindfold your guests (gently, no kidnapper energy) and give them small tastings of different chilli-laced items—sauces, dried chillies, spice blends. The goal? Identify the ingredients. The catch? One is mystery-level hot, and no one knows when it'll hit.

Keep a milk carton nearby like it's holy water and offer small prizes for correct guesses. Warning: some will cheat. Others will fake confidence. Everyone will bond over the shared trauma.

Fun Fact: Taste testing under blindfold actually intensifies flavour perception by heightening smell and texture awareness (Spence, 2015).

3. The One-Chip Challenge (a.k.a. The Hot Chip Horror Show)
Inspired by viral trends and one very evil tortilla chip, this is a solo gladiator game for your boldest guest, or for that one guy who says "nothing's ever spicy to me."

Offer them a single, certified weapon-grade chilli chip. No water. No milk. No rescue. Just one person, one chip, and five minutes of intense, regret-flavoured meditation.

Not for the faint of heart. But if filmed? Pure internet gold. And in group settings, this turns your event into legend.

According to Bryant et al. (2021), participants in spicy food challenges report adrenaline rushes and even a "runner's high," followed by sweaty regret. Worth it? You decide.

4. Chilli Roulette
Load up a tray of identical-looking foods—dumplings, truffles, cupcakes—where one or two are loaded with extra heat, and the rest are mild. Think of it as Russian roulette, but with more burping.

Guests take turns. Suspense builds. Laughter erupts. And suddenly, someone's got a mouthful of Carolina Reaper and zero coping skills.

Note: Make sure everyone consents and has emergency yoghurt nearby. Nobody wants their birthday party ending in a tongue lawsuit.

These chilli-fueled games are not just hilarious; they create connection. Everyone remembers the night they mistook ghost pepper jelly for strawberry jam. And as long as you provide tissues, ice cream, and a soft place to scream into a napkin, you'll be the talk of the town long after tongues cool down.

Decor, Costumes & Saucy Table Talk

So, you've nailed the spicy menu. You've got guests licking their lips, gulping cucumber coolers like they've seen a ghost, and fanning their faces with napkins. But now it's time for the true cherry on this chilli sundae—the vibe. Because food without flair is like a salsa dancer in slippers. Technically fine, but where's the razzle-dazzle?

Let's start with decor, the unsung hero of a memorable meal.

You don't need to remortgage your house to make your living room feel like a Thai night market or a New Orleans backyard. A few well-placed elements can do the trick. Think colour explosions—warm reds, yellows, deep oranges, or even metallics. These colours psychologically evoke heat and appetite (Spence, 2015). And no, I don't mean splattering sriracha on the walls. Use chilli garlands, paper lanterns, or even those mini fairy lights tucked into mason jars to create a sultry glow that whispers, "Yes, this is the party of the year."

Add in textures. A Mexican fiesta? Use embroidered cloths or serapes. Going East African? Woven baskets and bold patterns make a striking statement. Mood is a multisensory meal, and visuals are your spicy appetisers (Krishna, 2012).

Now let's talk costumes, because why just taste the world when you can wear it?

Encourage guests to dress in the spirit of your chosen chilli region. Someone shows up in a full kimono for your Gochujang night? Clap. A sombrero the size of a satellite dish? Offer extra salsa. These outfits don't just entertain; they deepen the connection between food and culture. It sparks questions, laughter, and maybe a few TikToks no one needs to see again. Dressing up increases emotional engagement and memory retention around events (Winterich et al., 2017). In plain English? People remember your party longer when they dressed like a Brazilian carnival float.

You can even take it further—chilli badges for winners of the tasting games, novelty aprons that say "Too Hot to Handle," or face stickers shaped like chillies. One party I went to handed out "Spice Survivor" headbands for people who made it through the hottest dish without milk. Iconic.

And now, the juiciest topic of all: saucy table talk.

This is where you, as the host, can make things unforgettable without lifting a skillet. Seed your table with conversation starters like:

- "What's the spiciest thing you've ever eaten, and survived?"
- "If you were a chilli, which one would you be?"
- "Would you rather bathe in hot sauce or spend a week with no seasoning at all?"

Watch people squirm, laugh, and bond. The goal is flavour in the mouth and fun in the air. You don't want a dinner party where everyone eats like they're at a tax audit.

You can even print mini chilli trivia cards with facts like:

- The ghost pepper is so hot it's used in elephant repellents in India.
- Capsaicin, the compound in chilli that causes heat, tricks your brain into thinking you're on fire.
- Chilli peppers are technically a fruit, just like tomatoes. Go figure.

This playful approach keeps conversation sizzling between bites. Just keep the tone fun, not a school quiz. It's dinner, not detention.

RING OF FIRE CHAMPIONSHIP
NO TEARS, JUST CHEERS
HOT
MILD
INSANITY
WAIVER FORM
CHILLI FIRE
MERCY CORNER
WARNING
KNOW YOUR SCOVILLE!

17 CHILLI EATING CONTESTS (WITHOUT ER VISITS)

"Life's too short to eat bland food," said someone brave, possibly shirtless, and definitely sweating from the ears.

And here we are. After whisking you through continents, condiments, and cocktails, it's time to crank up the heat and test the mettle of your spice-loving squad. But before we line up the reapers and ring the bell, let's address the habanero in the room: chilli contests are equal parts thrilling and terrifying, kind of like speed dating in a volcano.

This chapter is all about fun without fire department interventions. Because while watching your uncle Dave's soul evacuate his body mid-bite can be funny in theory, it stops being amusing when someone needs CPR between mouthfuls of Scotch Bonnets.

From heat level ladders to dare-based rewards, I'll walk you through how to host a chilli showdown that's unforgettable, for the right reasons. We're talking safety with spice, strategy with sizzle, and laughs with every face-melting bite.

So grab the milk, call the bravest of your brunch crew, and read on. Because by the end of this chapter, you'll be armed with everything you need to throw the hottest, safest, and most legendary heat-off in town.

Ready?

Let's fan the flames, responsibly.

How to Host a Safe & Fun Heat-Off

Welcome to the ring of fire, my friend. Not the Johnny Cash kind, but the kind where brave souls gather, mouths ablaze, sweat beading, and egos hanging by a ghost pepper thread. Before you throw your guests into the Scoville snake pit, let's make sure you're not secretly auditioning for "Jackass: The Dinner Party Edition."

You want laughs, not lawsuits. Thrills, not 999 calls. And definitely not a guest using your potted plant as a fire extinguisher. So let's spice things up with structure, sass, and just enough sanity to keep things fun.

1. The Golden Rule: Know Your Crowd
Before you bring out the Carolina Reapers, assess your guests like a bouncer at a VIP chilli club. Is this a crowd that giggles at Tabasco or drinks it like it's water? The goal is inclusive fire, not internal combustion.

You don't need everyone to be a chilli gladiator. Offer tiered challenges, from beginner jalapeño shots to boss-level ghost pepper bites. Create a heat ladder and let people choose their poison. No one likes peer pressure unless it's served with ranch dip and a side of applause (Ford et al., 2022).

2. Set the Rules and Actually Announce Them
Sounds obvious, but I've seen grown men forget the rules midway through a hot wing duel and end up nose-deep in a bowl of guacamole screaming, "Was this a trap?"

You need structure. Think rounds. Think rules. Think clearly labeled "this will kill your weekend" signs. And if you're serving alcohol? Set boundaries or risk the whole night becoming an accidental viral video (Kim & Patel, 2020).

Some smart rules to start with:

- No touching eyes (seriously).
- No heckling the cautious ones.
- Stop immediately if anyone goes full tomato-face or starts hiccuping like a haunted toaster.

3. Recruit a "Chilli Referee"
Every fire needs a firefighter. Nominate one guest to be the chilli sheriff, preferably someone who's sober, sensible, and not easily amused by suffering. Their job? Enforce breaks, monitor signs of heat distress, and offer tissues like a spicy guardian angel (Carter et al., 2021).

4. Stock the Safety Arsenal
You don't bring a firework and forget the extinguisher. Keep dairy, bread, honey, and bananas on standby. Avoid water; it's as useless as whispering at a

rock concert when it comes to chilli burn. And please, for the love of all things holy, label the lethal sauces clearly. No surprises.

5. Make the Prizes Wacky but Worth It
The winner doesn't need to get a gold medal. Make it funny. A crown of chillies. A "Lord of the Scoville" T-shirt. A tiny fire extinguisher trophy. Everyone should leave feeling like they won something, even if it's just bragging rights and a new respect for yoghurt.

6. Chill Stations & Crowd Camaraderie
Have a "cool-down zone" with icy towels, milkshakes, and soothing music. Make it feel like the chilli spa of redemption. Add a "confession booth" where participants can record dramatic monologues of their experience. Trust me, these will be the highlight of your after-party reel.

Heat Level Tiers & Progressions

Or: How Not to Accidentally Break Up a Friendship with One Bite of Bhut Jolokia

Let me say this loud enough for the people in the back, clutching their milk cartons like medieval shields: not all heat is created equal. A chilli eating contest without clear tiers is like karaoke night without a mic: chaos, screaming, and possibly someone crying in the bathroom.

Last section, we created the framework for a safe, fun heat-off. Now it's time to introduce the gladiators, ranked from the mild peasants to the fiery warlords. Because throwing a first-timer straight into ghost pepper territory is like enrolling a toddler in a judo class run by actual ninjas.

So, let's tier the heat like a sassy wedding cake: dramatic, layered, and possibly fatal if you don't pace yourself.

Tier 1: The Beginners' Baptism – Bell to Jalapeño

This is your "Welcome to the Heat" group. Think sweet bell peppers, banana peppers, poblano, and jalapeño. You're not breaking a sweat here. At worst, someone says, "Oooh, spicy," while reaching for another one five seconds later.

These are your warm-up acts, the spice equivalent of stretching before Zumba. Nobody earns a badge here, but it gives the crowd confidence and, more importantly, something to chew while judging the brave ones (Smith & Ortega, 2020).

Tier 2: The Mid-Level Mischief – Serrano to Thai Chilli

This tier is where flavor starts wearing brass knuckles. Serranos bring that sharp bite, like a sarcastic cousin at a family dinner. Thai chillies? Tiny but mighty. They show up dressed like candy but kick like Bruce Lee in a tutu.

Here's where lips tingle, nostrils flare, and the laughter gets that "I'm okay, I swear" waver. You need a sip of milk by round two, and a second opinion on your life choices by round three (Tan et al., 2021).

Tier 3: The Dangerous Darlings – Scotch Bonnet, Habanero, Bird's Eye

Enter the volcano gods. These chillies are colorful, cheerful-looking, and absolute liars. You'll sweat from places you didn't know had pores. Even your fingernails feel warm.

Scotch Bonnets bring fruity notes, right before they slap your soul. Habaneros dance on your tongue like a flamenco dancer with a vendetta. And bird's eye? That's the tiny red one that whispers, "I dare you," then ruins your Tuesday (Kwon & Delgado, 2019).

This is where brave souls begin hallucinating bargains with the spice gods. Make sure the cool-down station is in full view.

Tier 4: The Hellmouth – Ghost Pepper, Carolina Reaper, Dragon's Breath

If your party has reached this tier, either you've invited professional fire-eaters or you secretly hate your guests. This level is not for proving masculinity or peer pressure. This is for trained spice commandos or people going through a breakup and needing a symbolic burn.

Capsaicin levels here aren't just painful; they're record-breaking. The Carolina Reaper clocks in at over 2.2 million Scoville Heat Units (SHU). That's not food. That's weaponized agriculture. Have waivers. Have backup yoghurt. Have a will.

Mix it Up: The Wildcard Tier

Here's where things get spicy and strategic. Add twists: mystery chillies in unlabelled wrappers. Mix mild and hot bites like a culinary Russian roulette. Let participants spin a chilli wheel to determine their next level.

This adds fun unpredictability; just make sure the "wildcards" don't all come from the Devil's herb garden.

Guest Waivers (Just Kidding... Mostly)

If you read the last section and thought, "Wow, a chilli contest sounds fun!" congratulations, you're either incredibly brave or mildly unhinged. Either way, you're our kind of person.

But let me remind you: when you start dealing with Dragon's Breath chillies that literally require a hazmat warning in some countries, the line between fun and liability gets blurrier than your cousin's vision after licking a habanero on a dare.

So now, we ask the all-important question: do you need your guests to sign waivers? Technically, no. Practically, probably. Emotionally? Absolutely.

The Funny Fine Print of Friendship

Here's the deal. You probably don't need a lawyer. But if Uncle Dave insists on trying a whole Carolina Reaper "to prove a point," and then proceeds to breathe like a malfunctioning vacuum cleaner while screaming, "I'M FINE," you'll wish you had one.

This is why we joke about waivers, but kind of mean it.
A mock waiver is a hilarious, cheeky way to set the tone, lighten the mood, and remind guests they're voluntarily stepping into culinary battle. Think of it as the chilli lover's version of a bungee jump disclaimer. No one expects to die, but hey, we're acknowledging it's technically possible (Tan & Reynolds, 2021).

What to Include in a "Waiver" (Wink Wink)

You don't need a ten-page legal document. Keep it playful, but clear. Here's what your "just kidding… sort of" guest waiver might say:

- "I confirm I've willingly entered this event with a full stomach, a hydrated body, and questionable decision-making skills."
- "I understand that crying, hiccups, sweat, regret, and temporary ghost sightings may occur."
- "If I choose to consume a chilli from Tier 3 or 4, I do so knowing my taste buds may file for divorce."

Include a spot for their signature and emergency contact (even if it's just "Mum") and have fun with it. The point isn't legal protection; it's managing expectations, adding humour, and helping your guests mentally gear up for the burn (Rodriguez, 2019).

Real-World Example: The Reaper Wedding

A friend of mine, let's call him Leon, once hosted a chilli contest at his wedding. Why? Because nothing says romance like tongue-on-fire chaos. He printed a stack of satirical waivers titled "Sign Here If You're Willing to Risk Your Marriage for a Mango Ghost Chutney."

People laughed. They signed. And when one groomsman tried to play hero with a Trinidad Scorpion, the waiver made it clear: no one was dragging his spicy backside to the ER unless he gave them a ride home afterward.

Sometimes, comedy is your best insurance policy.

Gentle but Firm Boundaries

Now I know what you're thinking: "What if people just ignore the tiers and dive into the hottest stuff?" And that, my friend, is why clear boundaries are your spice-proof umbrella.

Print the heat tiers in giant, hilarious signs. Use colour codes. Put skull icons on anything over 1 million Scoville units. Maybe even have a referee. A dramatic one with a cape. Why not?

Also, don't let kids join the high-tier rounds, unless you want a very awkward phone call with someone's grandma. Set your rules early, post them everywhere, and stick to them (Liu et al., 2020).

A Little Peer Pressure Goes a Long Way

Let's be honest, half the fun of a chilli contest is watching confident people crumble dramatically in front of their peers. But pressure can be dangerous if it's not wrapped in good-natured humour.

Make it safe for people to tap out. Have a shame-free bell they can ring, like, "I'm out! My tongue just filed a restraining order!"

Celebrate participation, not survival. Award points for effort, courage, costume creativity, or funniest reaction. Keep the mood spicy, but not sinister.

Cooling Stations & Dare Rewards

You've made it through the flames, the tears, the minor identity crises caused by ghost peppers, and now, finally, we arrive at the oasis.
Cooling stations. The Switzerland of your chilli party. Neutral, safe, and absolutely necessary.

If the last section had us laughing over mock waivers and dramatised disclaimers, this one is about serious relief, and seriously clever rewards for those who dared to dance with the devils of spice.

Because if you're going to set mouths on fire, the least you can do is offer a friendly bucket of dairy and a pat on the back.

The Purpose of a Cooling Station (Hint: It's Not Just for the Weak)

Some people hear "cooling station" and picture a corner for quitters. Wrong. It's not a shame cave. It's a hospitality haven.

In every successful chilli challenge, there's a fine line between fun and 911. That line? It's lined with full-fat milk, ice cream, bread rolls, yoghurt tubs, cucumber slices, and, for the bougie among us, oat milk popsicles dusted with cardamom.

Research shows that dairy proteins like casein help break down the capsaicin oil responsible for the burning sensation (Kahkonen et al., 2019). Water just spreads the fire, like gossip at a family BBQ. But milk? Milk is your chilli-fighting superhero in liquid form (Bennett et al., 2020).

You're not being dramatic. You're being scientific.

Build Your Cooling Station Like a Spa Retreat, For the Tongue

Set up an area that feels inviting. Not sad. Not like a punishment corner in school. I'm talking:

- A "Chill Zone" sign written in blue icing font.
- Comfy seating—bean bags, picnic rugs, or even inflatable thrones (you earned it).
- Cooling towels in the fridge. No joke. You'll thank me when someone faceplants into one after a Carolina Reaper.
- Hydration jars with infused water (mint, lemon, cucumber).
- Cooling snacks: yoghurt parfaits, popsicles, ice cubes in fruit cups.

Think festival-meets-fridge. Add a speaker playing "Ice Ice Baby" if you must.

When in Doubt, Serve the Dairy

Now, if you've got guests who are lactose-intolerant, fear not. Coconut milk, almond milk, and oat milk can help, though not as effectively as dairy. Still, they're better than sending someone outside to cry under a sprinkler (Bajwa et al., 2021).

Always keep large bowls of:

- **Greek yoghurt** – Thick, rich, and soothing. Like a grandmother's hug for your taste buds.
- **Ice cream** – Bonus points if you make your own with chilli flakes for the brave.
- **Bread rolls and tortillas** – These help physically wipe capsaicin off the tongue. Also, carbs = comfort.
- **Honey** – Yes, honey! It coats the tongue like a warm blanket dipped in mercy.

Dare Rewards: Because Pain Deserves Prizes

Now onto the fun part. You've tortured your guests lovingly. Now it's time to reward their bravery. Think game show. Think epic. Think ridiculous.

Here are some spicy dare rewards to keep the fire spirits high:

1. **The Fire Breather Award** – For the contestant who powered through without a single tear. They get a golden chilli trophy or a T-shirt that says, "Tongue of Steel."

2. **The Drama Queen Crown** – For the most hilarious reaction. Bonus if they screamed and danced at the same time.
3. **The Comeback Kid Medal** – For someone who bailed early but came back swinging. A true chilli warrior arc.
4. **The Spice Whisperer Certificate** – For those who made it look way too easy. Probably a robot. But impressive nonetheless.

The point? Celebrate participation with the same heat you gave the contest. No one should leave empty-handed, even if their dignity stayed behind at Tier 2.

CREATE YOUR OWN HEAT!
SUNBURN SALSA
HOT SAUCE

18 DIY SAUCE BARS & GUEST SOUVENIR

You've come this far through the heat maze with me, so first, take a bow. Or better yet, take a shot of chilli-infused tequila (with consent, of course). By now, you've grilled, stirred, blended, and dared. You've wrangled Sriracha, danced with Scotch bonnets, and flirted with gochujang like a spice-slinging Casanova. So what's left?

Ah yes, souvenirs. Because if your guests leave your party with only mild heartburn and no keepsake, did the chilli gods really approve?

This chapter is all about bottling up memories, literally. Whether it's letting guests whip up their own lava-laced sauces or designing custom labels that say "I survived Lisa's Fire Fest 2025," you're about to learn how to turn your gathering into a gift shop of flaming joy.

You don't need to be Martha Stewart or Gordon Ramsay. You just need a sense of fun, a few mason jars, and a mild disregard for clean countertops.

By the end of this chapter, your guests won't just remember your party; they'll carry a piece of it home, wrapped in wax paper and tasting like delicious regret. Ready to get hands-on? Good. We're about to turn your kitchen into a chilli lab of love and laughter.

Make-Your-Own Hot Sauce Stations

Welcome to the sauce lab, where guests transform into mad scientists armed with aprons, tasting spoons, and enough chilli to clear sinuses on three continents. If you've ever wanted to make people cry with joy, of course, this is the moment. A DIY hot sauce station is the spicy equivalent of a wedding photo booth, except instead of duck lips and awkward props, you get habaneros, blenders, and bragging rights.

Now, before you imagine your kitchen looking like the aftermath of a paprika grenade, take a breath. With a few clever tweaks, this setup can be wildly fun and surprisingly tidy. Think salsa bar meets build-your-own adventure, with chilli.

Why You Need a DIY Sauce Station (Even if You're Not a "Host-y" Person)

Some folks throw parties with store-bought dips and Spotify playlists. But you? You're here to burn memories into tongues and brains. Literally. A make-your-own sauce bar adds interactive magic to your gathering. People mingle, swap ideas, whisper spicy secrets. Suddenly, Sharon from accounts is bonding with your cousin over scotch bonnets. It's social chemistry in action.

Research shows interactive food experiences increase guest satisfaction and connection (Sobal & Wansink, 2007). And let's be honest, folks are way more likely to remember your event if they left with their own custom bottle named "Fire in the Hole."

Your Simple, No-Fuss Setup

Let's keep this easy. You don't need an industrial kitchen or Gordon Ramsay's temper to pull this off.

Here's what you'll need:

- A clean table with wipeable cloths (trust me on this one)
- Food prep gloves
- Small glass bottles or jars (150ml works great)
- Funnels, spoons, and measuring jugs
- Blank labels and pens
- A blender or two (bullet-style or full-size)
- Bowls of chopped chillies (jalapeños, habaneros, Thai birds' eye, etc.)
- Vinegar (apple cider, white wine, or malt)
- Citrus (lemons and limes)
- Garlic, onion, salt, sugar, herbs, and optional fruit (mango, pineapple, strawberry for sweetness)

Set up a "base station" with the essentials: vinegar, citrus, and garlic.

Then let guests add chillies and fun extras like honey, ginger, or even dark chocolate. Encourage them to taste-test and tweak as they go.

Tips for Saucy Success

1. **Label everything:** From mild to murderously hot. You don't want a toddler accidentally spooning ghost pepper puree onto their chicken nugget.
2. **Provide a heat scale:** Use something visual, like a cartoon thermometer or emoji flames, to help people decide their spice destiny. The Scoville scale can be a fun reference too (Willet, 2015).
3. **Make a few pre-mixed examples:** Not everyone is brave. Give them inspiration, or a lifeline. Offer a mango-habanero blend, a smoky chipotle-garlic one, and a classic vinegar-based Louisiana style.
4. **Keep milk on hand:** Dairy is the ultimate fire extinguisher for capsaicin burn (Hoffman et al., 2016). Plant-based alternatives like oat milk work well too.
5. **Sanitation matters:** If someone dips a finger, that's not flavour; it's bacteria. Use tasting spoons and bin them after use.

The Naming Game

This is half the fun. Set up a label station with markers, stickers, and pun inspiration.

Examples:

- "Dragon's Breath Breakfast Blend"
- "Kiss of Regret"
- "Karen's Last Warning"
- "I Licked This Bottle First"

Guests take their labelled sauce home, and suddenly your house is a legend whispered about in office kitchens and barbecues across town.

Real-Life Spicy Story

At one party my cousin hosted, a guy named Lucas decided to toss every available chilli into one blender. "Go big or go bland," he declared. Twenty minutes later, he was pacing the patio, hiccupping uncontrollably, guzzling oat milk straight from the carton. The sauce? Delicious. But Lucas now speaks of it the way veterans speak of battle. It was named "Hell's Pajamas," and guests still ask me for the recipe.

Custom Heat Blends & Label Ideas

Some people collect stamps. Others brew beer in their garage. But you? You're about to become a full-fledged sauce alchemist, concocting blends so bold they could make a grown man weep into his tacos. If Make-Your-Own Hot Sauce Stations was the playground, this section is where the slide gets slick, the swings get turbo, and everyone's taking shots of vinegar like it's the new espresso.

If there's one thing I've learned from chilli parties (and yes, that's a real subculture), it's that the sauce isn't just about what's in the bottle. It's about what it says when it sits there, fiery and proud, next to someone's timid store-bought Tabasco.

You're not here for mild. You're here for identity, intensity, and something a little unhinged.

The Spice Matrix: Blend Profiles for Every Guest Archetype

When creating custom hot sauce blends, think like a DJ. You've got beats (heat), bass (body), and that little extra wobble (flavour note) that makes it unforgettable.

Here are four crowd-favourite profiles you can build your station around:

1. **The Sweet Assassin** – Mango + Scotch Bonnet + Honey + Lime.
   - Bright, fruity, and deceptively dangerous, like a tropical cocktail with a criminal record.
2. **The Smokeshow** – Chipotle + Roasted Garlic + Apple Cider Vinegar + Cumin.
   - For the guest who's wearing flannel and probably brought homemade jerky.
3. **The Green Dragon** – Jalapeño + Cilantro + White Vinegar + Green Apple.
   - Fresh, herby, and slightly feral. This one goes with everything.
4. **The Ferment Freak** – Red Thai Chillies + Fish Sauce + Ginger + Time.
   - Yep. Let this one age in a dark cupboard. Then wait for the funk to find you.

Each recipe is built around the idea that balance wins the race, even if that race is to see who can make Aunt Meryl sweat through her blouse. Capsaicin (the fire molecule) interacts with sweet, sour, and umami in powerful ways, creating complexity beyond the burn (McGee, 2004).

Flavor Notes = Power Moves

Encourage guests to pick a direction:

- Add fruit (pineapple, peach) for sweetness
- Add toasted spices (cumin, coriander, cinnamon) for depth
- Add fresh herbs (basil, mint) for a refreshing twist
- Add nuts or seeds (cashew, sesame) for creamy body

Don't just make sauce; make a statement. This is your hot-sauce fingerprint. Your chilli birthmark. Your legacy in a jar.

Label Like a Legend

A sauce without a label is like a tattoo with no backstory. Fun to look at, but missing its power.

Here's how to spark creativity:

- Set out blank kraft labels and permanent markers.
- Add a stack of hot-sauce name inspiration cards with ridiculous names like:
    - "Sir Sweats-a-Lot"
    - "Sneaky Heat"
    - "Don't Touch Your Eyes"
    - "Mildred's Midnight Regret"
- Offer pre-designed pun stickers or stamp kits for the artsy types.

  You can even create categories:

- **Fear Factor Blend:** "If Found, Do Not Taste"
- **Royal Heat:** "Crown Me With Carolina Reaper"
- **Chill Charmer:** "Cool... Until It's Not"

Encourage inside jokes. "Keith's Kryptonite." "Blair's Bad Decisions." Suddenly, your event becomes unforgettable, because the sauces are talking.

According to consumer psychology, customization increases emotional attachment and perceived value (Franke, Schreier & Kaiser, 2010). Translation? A guest is way more likely to remember, and post about, your party if they leave with a bottle they named and built themselves.

Real-Life Sizzle

My neighbour once threw a chilli-themed baby shower (yes, spicy diapers were involved). One guy named his bottle "Infant Inferno" and gave a toast about how heat builds resilience. Another lady made a pink label called "Rosy Rumbler" and gifted it to the mum-to-be. Guess what? It's still in her fridge, untouched, but sacred.

That's what a great label does. It turns sauce into story.

Takeaway Jars & Spice Gift Bags

You know that feeling when your guests are leaving, still licking their fingers and already dreaming of the hot sauce they just demolished with your triple-smoked jalapeño wings? Yeah, that moment is the golden window. The "Can I take some home?" moment. And if you're like me, you don't want to be caught scraping leftover sauce into a takeaway coffee cup like a sad food hoarder at midnight.

Enter: Takeaway jars and spice gift bags. Your spicy exit strategy.

Now, I'm not talking about mass-producing artisanal jars with wax seals and a "handcrafted in Tuscany" label (unless you've got a Nonna with a warehouse and a team of interns). I'm talking fun-sized glass jars, the kind you find at dollar stores or online in bulk, filled with your signature sauce and labelled with enough personality to make Gordon Ramsay blush.

Real Talk: One friend of mine labelled her peach-habanero sauce: "Peach Please, You Can't Handle This Heat." Another called his garlic chilli paste "Dragon's Breath for Breakfast." Your label doesn't need to be perfect; it just needs to speak. Loudly. Like your uncle after two beers and one bite of ghost pepper dip.

Pro tip: Use waterproof labels, or you'll end up handing out jars that look like they went through a toddler's bath time. Sites like Avery, Canva, or even Amazon offer pre-cut sticker templates that are easy to customise (Avery, 2023; Canva, 2024).

And what's a good hot sauce without a little flair? Tie a mini wooden spoon or a chillified recipe tag to the lid using twine or raffia. Instant upgrade. People lose their minds over thoughtful touches, especially when they're edible, flammable, or both.

Now let's talk spice gift bags. Because not everyone wants to leave with a liquid time bomb in their handbag. Some guests just want to dabble, not drown.

You can fill these bags with:

- Mini sachets of your dry rubs (hello, cumin-chilli-lime magic),
- Dehydrated chilli flakes (labelled "Volcano Dust", obviously),
- Or custom spice blends with themes like "Taco Tuesday Saver" or "Sunday Roast Wake-Up Call."

You know what else makes it gold? Personal notes. A quick scribble that says: "Warning: This dust bit my brother. He still cries during thunderstorms." Funny. Memorable. Legal coverage.

According to event planners, souvenir gifts that reflect the party's flavour, literally and emotionally, are 78% more likely to be remembered (Smith, 2020). And if that means your cousin Barry is talking about your habanero honey glaze for the next five years, so be it.

Bonus idea: Wrap everything in brown craft paper stamped with chilli emojis or fun slogans like "Caution: Contents May Ruin Weak Tongues". Presentation matters. Because no one remembers the soggy napkin you gave them. But they will remember the bag that said "Fire in a Pouch."

Oh, and a quick tip for you spicy soul bosses running short on time: Set up a "Pack Your Own Fire" station at the end of your party. Lay out empty jars, a filling spoon, labels, pens, stickers, and a menu card of what's in each jar. People LOVE customisation. It's like Build-A-Bear, but for adults who think jalapeños are a personality.

If you've made it this far, congrats, you're officially the chilli fairy godparent your friends didn't know they needed. But let's not have them walk out of your spicy soirée empty-handed like it was just a free tasting session at a grocery store. No, no. You've built memories, fanned flames, and now it's time to send your guests home with something that screams, "You survived. You earned this."

Welcome to the magical world of takeaway jars and spice gift bags.

You know how weddings have those awkward little thank-you trinkets? Candied almonds in organza bags, or a magnet shaped like the couple's initials? Cute. But your chilli gathering deserves something with a bit more punch, literally.

Custom Jars: Mini But Mighty

Grab a set of 4oz glass jars with screw-top lids (bonus if they're tinted amber like tiny apothecary bottles of fire). Fill each with your signature hot sauce from the night, and slap on a bold label. Call it "Uncle Tony's Tongue Twister" or "Midnight Sweat No. 7." Add heat warnings. Add a ridiculous backstory. Have fun with it.

Not sure where to begin with labeling? Canva's free templates are a game-changer, especially for the design-impaired among us (Canva, 2024). And if you want those labels waterproof, because some people refrigerate with enthusiasm, use weatherproof printable sticker sheets from brands like Avery (Avery, 2023).

You can also personalize heat levels with little colour-coded dots. Red for "call the fire brigade," yellow for "my tongue's tingling," and green for "barely a sizzle, Karen."

Gift Bags: A Tiny Explosion of Joy

Now, don't just hand out a jar like a baked bean sample. Presentation matters. Use kraft paper bags or mini burlap sacks. Tie them up with a raffia bow, and tuck in:

- A mini wooden spoon (for elegant dabbing).
- A heat-level card explaining the Scoville range.
- A recipe suggestion using the sauce (like "drizzle on scrambled eggs for a divorce-worthy breakfast.")

And yes, include a "thank you for being spicy" tag. If you're feeling especially extra, throw in a chilli-shaped eraser or hot sauce keychain. The point is, this is your edible business card, a souvenir people will remember long after the burn fades.

Optional Add-Ons for Overachievers

Want to win the imaginary "Host of the Year" trophy? Consider these spicy extras:

1. **Infused Salts** – Mix flaky sea salt with chilli powder and lime zest. Bag it in mini vials labeled "Witch's Sprinkle."
2. **Chilli Oil Samplers** – Use dropper bottles (yes, the kind used for beard oil) filled with infused chilli oils: garlic-chilli, ginger-sesame, or lemon-coriander.
3. **Taster Packs** – Scoop out 1 tsp of 3–4 different hot sauces or spice rubs into little condiment containers. Call it your "Heat Flight."

Why This Works (According to Science)

Research shows that memorable food experiences are enhanced by strong sensory cues and takeaway elements that extend the memory into the home (Spence, 2015). When your guests use that hot sauce a week later, they're not just eating; they're time-traveling back to the laughter, the fire, the games. That's hospitality magic.

And honestly, it's way more useful than another coaster set or scented candle.

So, friend, don't let your guests stumble out of your chilli party with nothing but scorched taste buds and fond memories. Hand them a jar. Gift them a grin. Leave them with a little bit of burn in their bag and a whole lot of love in their heart.

N
W
W
S
BEWARE OF
EVIL SPIRITS
HAIR GROWTH
POTION
LOVE SPELL
THE GLOBAL MYTHS OF THE FIERY PEPPER

19 CHILLI MYTHS, LORE & TRIVIAL TIDBITS

Mark Twain once said, "Never let the truth get in the way of a good story." And honestly, when it comes to chillies, people have taken that advice and run with it like their pants were on fire.

Welcome to the spice rack of superstition, the folklore aisle of your mental supermarket. This chapter is not about recipes; it's about the weird, the wild, and the absolutely-who-started-that nonsense people believe about chillies around the world. We've danced with dishes, battled buffalo wings, and sweat through sambals, but now, we're shifting gears into the bizarre and delightful carnival of chilli legends.

From ancient Aztec warriors who thought chillies scared off evil spirits (and maybe nosy in-laws), to modern TikTokers who believe rubbing pepper on your scalp will grow hair faster, this chapter is equal parts myth-busting and laugh-spitting. You'll come away with just enough spicy trivia to impress your next dinner date or ruin a perfectly peaceful meal with unnecessary facts.

Let's toast to the chilli, not just as a fruit (yes, it's a fruit!) but as a global mischief-maker that has inspired superstition, sparked revolutions, and burned its way into the pages of culinary folklore.

Weird Chilli Superstitions & Beliefs

Now, I don't know who needs to hear this, but rubbing a chilli pepper on your baby's forehead will not protect them from evil spirits. It will, however, result in one angry baby and possibly a call from child services.

Welcome to the spicy underworld of chilli superstitions, where fact checks take a backseat and folklore grabs the wheel, swerving wildly through culture, tradition, and occasionally pure nonsense.

Let's kick off in India, where chillies aren't just for cooking; they're for exorcisms. Ever seen a string of green chillies and lemons hanging from a shop or taxi? That's not a DIY air freshener. It's called "nimbu-mirchi", a charm meant to ward off the evil eye and bring prosperity. The belief is that the sourness of the lemon and the heat of the chilli together create a hostile environment for bad spirits. Which makes sense; nothing evil wants heartburn and citrus in its eyes (Chakraborty, 2021).

Then there's Mexico, a land where chilli is practically a religion. But here's the twist: some folks believe that pregnant women who eat too many chillies will birth babies with fiery tempers. This may sound absurd, but it's a surprisingly common warning passed from abuelas to their daughters. The belief is part moral caution, part dietary advice, and part, "don't come crying to me when your kid grows up yelling at the microwave" (Pilcher, 2012).

Meanwhile, in Thailand, certain farmers won't plant chillies on specific days tied to lunar phases because it's said to bring bad luck or stunt the plant's growth. And in some African cultures, sprinkling chilli powder near a doorway is believed to keep away intruders, not just the two-legged kind, but spiritual ones too. Apparently, ghosts, much like uninvited guests, really hate capsaicin.

But wait, it gets weirder.

In the Philippines, some believe chillies can attract love if you burn a dried pod and let the smoke waft toward your crush. Nothing says "I'm into you" like the smell of scorched chilli and potential smoke inhalation.

And don't get me started on the beauty hacks. In some online wellness corners (looking at you, DIY beauty TikTok), chilli-infused oils are promoted as miracle cures for hair regrowth. The theory is that capsaicin increases blood flow to the scalp, stimulating follicles. The reality? You'll mostly just irritate your scalp and smell like a spicy stir-fry (Ravikumar & Kathirvel, 2020). But hey, at least you'll be memorable on dates.

What ties all of this together is the chilli's dual nature. It's medicine and mayhem. It heals and harms. It invites and protects. In cultures worldwide, it's more than food; it's a symbol. Of protection, of power, of passion, and sometimes, of completely illogical, but wildly entertaining, beliefs.

And while I personally wouldn't recommend any of these as scientifically sound practices (seriously, don't pepper-bomb your crush), I do think they reveal something beautiful: chillies have embedded themselves into human ritual, not just as flavour but as folklore. And any ingredient that spicy deserves to live a little larger than life.

Historical Heat: The Story of Chillies

Let's rewind the spice clock. Long before Sriracha met scrambled eggs and before Tabasco found fame in MREs and frat houses, there was a humble fruit quietly plotting world domination: the chilli pepper.

Now, if chillies had a theme song, it'd be *Started from the bottom, now we're here.* Because truly, they started modest, wild, untamed, and blazing their way across the Americas over 6,000 years ago. Archaeological finds in Mexico's Tehuacán Valley show that early humans were already domesticating chillies around 4,000 BCE, well before they got around to corn or beans (Pickersgill, 2007). Priorities, clearly.

The ancient Aztecs and Mayans didn't just eat chillies; they worshipped them. In Aztec culture, chillies were so hot they could literally offend the gods, so they fasted from them during certain rituals (Smith, 2001). They also used chillies as currency, medicine, and even weapons. Yes, weapons. Picture this: ancient warriors burning chilli pods to create a kind of spicy smoke bomb to choke enemies. Primitive pepper spray. Talk about blazing trails.

But here's where the story explodes, like biting into a ghost pepper without warning. Enter: Christopher Columbus.
Columbus sailed west looking for India and its precious black pepper. Instead, he stumbled upon the Caribbean and found the chilli. Naturally, he misnamed it "pepper" because it was spicy and he was confused. (Classic Columbus, wrong directions, wrong names, still gets the credit.) He hauled the chilli back to Europe, unknowingly kickstarting the global spice trade's most fiery chapter.

From Europe, chillies spread like juicy gossip at a family reunion, unstoppable. Portuguese traders carried them to Africa and Asia, where they were embraced like long-lost relatives. India, in particular, went absolutely wild for chillies. Within a century of their arrival, chillies had dethroned long-standing native spices and claimed their place in curries and chutneys (Bosland & Votava, 2012).

And then came China. The Sichuan province, now globally known for its numbing heat, didn't even meet the chilli until the 1600s. But once they did, they married it with Sichuan peppercorns and created one of the most iconic, face-melting flavor combos of all time. Culinary history was officially on fire.

In Africa, chillies adapted and evolved, becoming central to the continent's signature sauces and stews, like the fiercely loved piri-piri in Mozambique and Angola. Traders might've introduced the chilli, but locals made it legendary.

Fast-forward to today, and chillies are everywhere. They're not just food;

they're identity. They define cuisines, fuel national dishes, and spark heated debates over who makes the best hot sauce. (Spoiler: everyone thinks it's their grandma.)

And let's not forget the science. Chillies owe their heat to capsaicin, a sneaky little compound that binds to pain receptors in your mouth and tricks your brain into thinking you're on fire. But oddly enough, your body loves the chaos. That burning feeling? It triggers endorphins. So technically, loving chillies is a form of legal masochism (Kobata, 2014).

The chilli's journey from wild shrub to global superstar is one of survival, spice, and spicy survival. It crossed oceans, rewrote cuisines, and burned its way into our history, hearts, and mouths.

And I don't know about you, but next time I drizzle hot sauce on a taco, I'll whisper a quiet "thank you" to the chilli rebels who came before me.

Fun Facts to Drop at Dinner Parties

Let's face it, every dinner party has That One Guest. The one who waits for the perfect moment to drop a fact so unexpected, so outrageously spicy, it silences the table. What if I told you… that could be YOU?

Welcome to your arsenal of chilli facts. So good, they'll earn you second helpings and shocked gasps. I mean, why talk weather when you could talk Scovilles, sweat glands, and exploding curry competitions?

Fact #1: The world's hottest pepper could be used as a weapon.

The Carolina Reaper holds the Guinness World Record for hottest chilli, clocking in at over 2.2 million Scoville Heat Units (SHU) (Guinness World Records, 2023). That's basically pepper spray for your tongue. In fact, in India, the Defence Research Lab even experimented with using Bhut Jolokia (Ghost Pepper) in grenades for riot control (CNN, 2010). So yes, you could technically fight crime with curry.

Fact #2: Chillies are fruit. Yes, fruit.

I know. It sounds like a nutritional betrayal. But botanically speaking, chillies grow from a flower and contain seeds, just like tomatoes and avocados. So the next time someone offers you "fruit salad," feel free to chuck in a habanero and act smug.

Fact #3: Eating chillies can help you live longer.

Science says spice might just be your passport to longevity. A massive 2015 study published in *The BMJ* found that people who consumed spicy food regularly had a 14% lower risk of death compared to their bland-food counterparts (Lv et al., 2015). So yes, that burning sensation might just be adding years to your life. Who knew pain was the fountain of youth?

Fact #4: There's a phobia of spicy food.

It's called capsaicinophobia, the irrational fear of hot peppers or spicy food. Symptoms include sweating at the sight of salsa and avoiding people who carry sriracha in their bags. If that's you, don't worry, we still love you. Just don't come near my nachos.

Fact #5: Chilli eating is now a competitive sport.

From YouTube challenges to chilli festivals, there's a global underground of brave souls who train their mouths like Olympic athletes. Some train their taste buds by gradually increasing heat levels. Others? They skip straight to Reaper roulette. There's even a League of Fire, where people earn points for surviving brutal spicy challenges (League of Fire, 2022). Somewhere in the world, someone is crying for views.

Fact #6: Chillies have travelled to space.

Yes, NASA astronauts grew chilli peppers on the International Space Station, specifically the Española Improved variety. Why? Because nothing says "conquering space" like a taco with heat. Astronaut Megan McArthur even tweeted about making space tacos, which should be in a museum, honestly (NASA, 2021).

Fact #7: Chilli sweat is a thing, and it's a compliment.

It's called gustatory sweating, and it happens when your nervous system confuses spice with heat and says, "Better sweat this out before we combust." The more it burns, the more you sweat, and in some cultures, sweating at a meal is a sign of appreciation. So mop your forehead with pride.

Fact #8: Chillies have moods. Kind of.

Capsaicin isn't distributed equally across every chilli. One jalapeño might kiss you gently, while its sibling shanks you with heat. This inconsistency led to the term "chilli roulette", a party game where only one stuffed pepper is secretly loaded with a hot one. It's food, it's Russian roulette, and it's hilarious until you're the victim.

World Records & Chilli Hall of Fame

Let me take you behind the velvet rope, into a spicy hall where the ceilings drip with hot sauce and the statues are carved out of dried chillies. This is where legends live. The brave. The burping. The slightly unhinged.

Welcome to the Chilli Hall of Fame, where pain meets glory and the records are hotter than your auntie's stew after a breakup.

Record #1: The Hottest Chilli in the World (and Still Holding Court)

As of the last count by the Guinness World Records, the Carolina Reaper holds the crown, boasting a brain-melting 2.2 million Scoville Heat Units (SHU) (Guinness World Records, 2023). That's about 880 times hotter than a jalapeño. Grown by Ed Currie in South Carolina, this pepper isn't just hot; it's the devil's perfume.

People have passed out. Vomited. Sworn off spice for life. And yet... we keep buying it.

Record #2: Most Chillies Eaten in One Minute

Let's pause and honour Gregory Foster, who devoured 17 Ghost Peppers (Bhut Jolokia) in 60 seconds. That's not a snack. That's a therapy session waiting to happen. The Ghost Pepper used to hold the world's hottest record, so this feat isn't just speed; it's survival (BBC News, 2022).

I don't know what's more impressive: his mouth or his health insurance.

Record #3: World's Largest Chilli Pepper Collection

There's a man in the UK, let's call him the Indiana Jones of Spice, who owns over 500 varieties of chillies from around the globe. That's not a pantry. That's a museum. His collection includes rare varieties like the Chocolate Scorpion and the Zimbabwe Bird Eye (UK Chilli Association, 2021).

Imagine trying to label those jars without making it sound like a crime report.

Record #4: Most People Eating Chillies Simultaneously

In 2017, 1,446 people gathered in Mexico City and bit into chillies together, setting the world record for the largest simultaneous chilli tasting (Guinness World Records, 2017). You can practically hear the collective gasp from space.

Why do we do this to ourselves? Because somewhere between the sear and the sweat, we become superheroes. Or at least, very brave fools with numb tongues.

Record #5: Longest Chilli Sausage

Because why not? In Italy, food artisans created a 597-metre-long spicy sausage infused with Calabrian chillies. That's longer than five football fields, and enough to make every vegetarian within 50 miles spontaneously combust.

Imagine trying to flip that on a grill. You'd need a team of firemen, a forklift, and a prayer.

Hall of Fame Inductees: Legends of the Flame

- **Smokin' Ed Currie** – Creator of the Carolina Reaper and all-around spice sorcerer. The man grows chillies like he's feeding dragons.

- **Padma Lakshmi** – Not just a host, but a spice ambassador. Her shows have brought global heat into living rooms around the world.
- **The Chilli Queens of San Antonio** – Back in the 1800s, these Mexican-American women sold chilli from open-air stalls in Texas and kickstarted America's love affair with chilli con carne. Legends before it was cool.

But Let's Get Real: Not All Heroes Wear Bibs

There's a grandma in Nigeria who makes stew so hot, it has to be served with a verbal disclaimer. There's a street vendor in Bangkok who serves noodles that make grown men cry. These are the unsung heroes. The everyday heat whisperers.

They may never hold a Guinness title, but they own their block.

And with that, we close the curtain on chilli legends. But before you hang up your apron and toss out your spice rack, pause. We're not done just yet.

Up next: a soft landing to this wild ride in Chapter 20, where we cool things down, reflect on your new superpowers, and send you out into the world armed with heat, humour, and a whole lot of flavour. Let's finish strong.

Sunburn Salsa
Smoky Inferno
Guest Souvenir
THE CHILLI LEGACY
Keep the flame alive.

20 THE FINAL SPELL – ENTERTAINING WITH HEART, HEAT & HUMOUR

"Laughter is brightest in the place where the chilli burns the tongue… or something like that." – Probably someone's grandma

You made it. Through cayenne chaos, salsa stand-offs, and sambal seductions, you've survived 19 full-flavoured chapters. If this book had a loyalty card, you'd be owed a free bottle of milk and a personal fire extinguisher. So first, thank you. Not just for reading, but for committing to bringing spice to your life, your kitchen, and the souls of those brave enough to eat your food.

Now, we're not wrapping up like some boring boardroom meeting with polite claps and lukewarm coffee. No ma'am. We're ending with fire, flair, and a farewell so fabulous it'll leave your pantry weeping tears of ghost pepper joy.

This final chapter is the confetti cannon of your chilli journey. We're talking signature heat styles, how to be a next-level chilli host, and yes, even a dramatic curtain call worthy of the Sorceress herself.

Grab your ladle. It's time to stir one last spell.

Finding Your Signature Heat Style

You know how some folks have a signature dance move? That thing they whip out at weddings when "September" by Earth, Wind & Fire kicks in and dignity leaves the room? Well, it turns out chilli lovers have signature moves too. Except ours are edible, unpredictable, and might require aloe vera after.

This section is about you, your chilli identity, your spicy alter ego, your flavour fingerprint. Because not all fire is forged equal, darling.

Let's go back.
Remember Chapter 3 when we experimented with chilli desserts and half of you were suspicious? "Who puts jalapeño in cheesecake?" you asked. Now here you are, secretly Googling "ghost pepper gelato" and wondering if your mother-in-law can handle it. Growth, my friend. Growth.

But here's the twist: being a chilli sorcerer isn't about maxing out the Scoville scale and seeing who cries first. It's about intention. Do you stir with love? Garnish with mischief? Do you aim to soothe or seduce, sting or surprise?

The Four Spicy Archetypes
After years of taste tests, burnt tongues, and therapy (mostly from my poor dinner guests), I've narrowed it down to four spicy archetypes. See where you fit:

1. **The Steady Sizzle**
   You believe flavour > fire. You're the one blending mild Kashmiri chilli into tomato sauces or reaching for a smoked paprika instead of a Carolina Reaper. You're all about depth. No drama, no trauma. Just flavour that hums like a well-tuned jazz trio.
   - **Chilli bestie:** Aleppo pepper. Smoky, sweet, approachable. Just like you.
   - **Signature move:** Slow-roasted comfort with a whisper of warmth.
2. **The Mischievous Flame**
   You like surprises. One minute your guests are calmly enjoying dinner, the next they're fanning their faces like Baptist aunties at a summer sermon. You don't aim to cause harm; you just enjoy watching mild chaos unfold.
   - **Chilli bestie:** Thai bird's eye or scotch bonnet.
   - **Signature move:** Hidden heat bombs in an otherwise innocent dish.
3. **The Elegant Ember**
   You're a flavour stylist. Your chilli use is refined, minimalist, and intentional, like adding a silk scarf to an outfit. You prefer infused oils, chilli flakes in honey, or a single strand of dried chilli curling on a burrata plate. Your food whispers sophistication while still warming the soul.
   - **Chilli bestie:** Urfa Biber or Gochugaru.
   - **Signature move:** A finishing drizzle of fire that feels like a

wink across the table.

4. **The Heat Healer**
   You use chilli like a potion, something that wakes up the senses, heals what's sluggish, and reconnects people around the table. Your food doesn't scream; it sings in harmony. Think turmeric-laced chilli broths or ginger-chilli tonics.
   - **Chilli bestie:** Serrano, cayenne, or crushed long red chillies.
   - **Signature move:** Spicy soups, health-forward stews, or medicinal sauces with character.

According to research from the University of Pennsylvania, individuals who enjoy spicy food often associate it with thrill-seeking and emotional release, which makes sense if your signature dish has brought a grown man to tears… twice (Rozin et al., 2013).

Another study found that capsaicin, the compound that gives chillies their heat, triggers endorphins and dopamine, giving you that "spicy high" (Noling, 2020). So yes, that smile after hot wings is not just pride. It's science.

And let's not forget: culture shapes our chilli behaviour too. A 2022 global flavour trend report showed that chilli preferences correlate with geography, tradition, and even personality type (Innova Market Insights, 2022). Basically, where you grew up might explain why you carry hot sauce in your handbag like it's perfume.

So, which one are you?

Maybe you're a hybrid. A Steady Sizzle by day, Elegant Ember by dinner party. Maybe you're a full-blown Mischievous Flame who thrives on watching friends reach for ice cubes mid-meal. Either way, own it. Declare it. Frame it if you must.

Your chilli identity isn't just what you cook; it's how you host, how you play, how you bring people together. It's a spice-soaked extension of who you are.

So go ahead, write your chilli legacy in sauce and steam.

How to Be a Chilli Host with the Most

Some people host dinner parties. You start edible riots, with charm, cheer, and chilli-laced chaos. And if you're reading this thinking, "Wait, me? A chilli host?" oh yes, you. You've made it this far. You've braved sambals and sorbets. You've dabbled in Harissa, flirted with Gochujang, and tangoed with scotch bonnets like a salsa dancer in a spice market.

Hosting with chilli is not for the faint of heart. It's for the generous, the daring, and the slightly unhinged in the most lovable way. Let's sharpen your skills and crown you Host of the Heat Realm.

Step One: Know Thy Guests (and Their Guts)

Look, not everyone wants to eat a Carolina Reaper and hallucinate their ancestors. Respect the thresholds.

Have a short conversation before the party (or a cheeky questionnaire if you're the Excel-loving type). Ask about spice tolerance, allergies, or that one cousin who cries at the sight of sriracha.

Hot Tip: Create a 3-tiered menu:

- **Mild but Mighty** (flavour-packed without fire)
- **Medium Mischief** (tingle without trauma)
- **Flamin' Foolery** (for your ride-or-die spice heads)

According to the British Nutrition Foundation, spicy food is enjoyed best when eaten in comfort, not terror (BNF, 2021). Translation: don't ambush people with habaneros unless they consent to the madness.

Step Two: Create a Sensory Experience, Not a Food Fling

Being a Chilli Host with the Most means you're not just feeding mouths; you're creating a memory. Light incense that smells like smoky chipotle. Play music that matches the vibe—Afrobeat for Peri-Peri, Thai pop for bird's eye basil stir-fry, or classic soul while stirring chilli con carne.
Every bite should tell a story. Every sauce should say something.

And keep things interactive! Have a sauce bar. Do a DIY taco station. Let people add their heat level like spice DJs spinning Scoville records.
As chef and spice advocate Nik Sharma says, "A good host doesn't just feed you. They surprise you, inspire you, and teach you something new" (Sharma, 2020).

Step Three: Emergency Protocols (The Sexy Kind)

Let's get real. Someone's going to overdo it. They'll be trying to impress their date or win a dumb dare. Suddenly, they're sweating like a sinner in church.
You, dear host, must be ready.
Stock up on yoghurt, milk, rice, and maybe a handheld fan. Avoid water; it's like trying to put out a fire with gasoline. Capsaicin is oil-soluble, so dairy's your superhero here (Garcia, 2022).

Keep humour handy too. "Congratulations! You've unlocked the 'Overconfident Guest Achievement Badge.' Your prize? Coconut milk and an ice cube to the forehead."
And please, label everything. That sweet tomato chutney might actually be a

ghost pepper ambush in disguise. Don't lose friends over false advertising.

Step Four: Leave Them Talking (and Breathing)

You want guests to leave saying, "I've never had anything like that before," not "I may never taste food again."
So finish with flair:

- A mild chilli-laced dessert (think chocolate and cayenne truffles)
- A take-home sauce jar with their name on it
- A handwritten note with their "heat rating" of the night, completely subjective, of course

Celebrate the drama. Honour the survivors. Praise the ones who tapped out early but still showed up for seconds.

Being a chilli host isn't about perfection. It's about personality. Precision. And a pinch of planned pandemonium.

Because the real secret of great hosting? You don't just feed people; you enchant them.

A Thank-You Note to My Guests (and Tongues)

Dear brave tongue-bearers, spice lovers, and unintentional fire-breathers,

Let's get straight to it: YOU are the real MVPs.

You came. You crunched. You cried. And still, you asked for seconds.

So, before I unleash my final blessing in this spellbook of sizzling memories, I owe you this one heartfelt, hiccup-filled THANK YOU. Because every wild party, every perfectly charred pepper, every moment where someone shouted, "WHY IS THIS SO HOT BUT SO GOOD?", only works because of guests like you. Mad, magnificent, and marinated in love.

You Didn't Just Show Up. You Showed Out.

You could've stayed home with your usual pasta and polite conversation. But no. You chose fire over comfort. Flavour over fear. You RSVP'd to madness, wore stretchy pants, and risked your tastebuds for something unforgettable.

If this were a sport, you'd be in the Spicy Olympics. And I'd be handing out medals shaped like jalapeños dipped in glitter.

Even the quiet ones who sipped water between every bite, respect. Because spice is a personal journey. And just showing up to a chilli party? That's the start of legend status.

You Made the Kitchen Feel Like a Stage

Ever hosted a chilli night and watched the room transform?

One second, everyone's politely buttering toast. The next, someone's explaining the Scoville scale using interpretive dance, another is crying into a tortilla, and someone else is live-streaming their "habanero experience" to TikTok.

You, dear guest, brought the vibe. The chaos. The comedy. And the sense of collective adventure that made the chilli more than just food; it became the glue. The giggle. The dare. The memory.

As food anthropologist Sarah Lohman puts it, "We remember the meals not just for what was eaten, but for who we became while eating them" (Lohman, 2016). In this case? Brave. Bold. Slightly unhinged.

You Also Forgave Me for the Scorching

Let's be honest: some of those dishes were borderline criminal. The "mild" mango salsa that secretly housed serranos? Yeah… about that.
And still, you smiled. You swore. You probably cursed my name in three languages and kept chewing. THAT, my friend, is loyalty.

A 2020 survey by *Hot Sauce Magazine* (yes, that exists) revealed that 72% of people actually enjoy the endorphin rush from spicy food, even when it hurts a little (Hot Sauce Mag, 2020). It's pain with a purpose. And I'm honoured you trusted me with your tongue.

To the Tongues, Let Us Salute You

Let's take a moment of silence for all the tastebuds who didn't make it.
To the tongues that tingled, to the ones that tapped out and said, "Nope, not today,", thank you for being the frontline soldiers. You're the unsung heroes behind the burps, the bravery, and the burning but beautiful bites.

May your nerve endings regenerate in time for the next round.
And if you lost a few along the way? That's the price of glory, my friend.

You Turned a Meal into Magic

This isn't just a thank-you note; it's a chilli-stained love letter. Because when guests show up with open hearts, curious mouths, and just enough mischief to say, "I'll try it," the meal becomes a memory.

You made this book, this journey, this madness possible.

And while I may have hosted the party, YOU brought the party to life.
So, from the bottom of my spice-loving heart… thank you. For letting me roast your tastebuds, tickle your humour, and take you around the globe one pepper at a time.

Now go moisturise your lips. Drink some milk. And get ready.
Because if you're still standing after this? You're not just a guest.
You're family now.

The Chilli Sorceress's Final Blessing

There's a moment, right after the plates are cleared, the laughter has softened, and someone's still fanning their tongue with a coaster, when you realise: this wasn't just a meal. It was a ritual.

And you were part of it. Now, my fiery friend, as we wrap up this rollicking roast of a cookbook, it's time for the final incantation. A blessing, not the holy water kind, but the hot sauce variety. The one that sticks to your ribs, your memory, and hopefully your apron.

"One cannot think well, love well, sleep well, if one has not dined well." – Virginia Woolf, a woman who surely would've dipped her quill in chilli oil if given the chance.

So, What Does This Blessing Look Like?

First, I don't bestow blandness. I don't hand out certificates of culinary politeness. What I give is fire with purpose. Joy with flavour. Chaos that's welcome at the table.

This isn't a cookbook for people who want to impress with precision. This is for the glorious rebels, the chilli-smeared heroes who cook with instinct and laugh mid-recipe. This is for YOU.

So here is my three-fold blessing. Use it. Frame it. Tattoo it on your kitchen wall if you must.

1. May Your Heat Always Match Your Heart
There's no shame in being a jalapeño in a room full of ghost peppers. Whether you're mild, medium, or straight-up infernal, own it. Your flavour is enough.

In fact, studies show that people's spice tolerance is linked to their personality—risk-takers tend to crave higher heat, while those who enjoy control lean mild (Byrnes & Hayes, 2013). But guess what? There's no prize for the spiciest soul, only for the most authentic one.

So, whether you're sautéing Scotch bonnets or gently coaxing heat from paprika, do it with intention. Do it with pride. Do it with a grin and an apron stained with yesterday's sauce.

2. May Your Kitchen Be Your Playground (and Your Lab)
Chilli cooking is half mischief, half magic. Don't get stuck in what worked once. Try weird combos. Set up blind taste tests. Infuse oil with lemongrass and dare someone to guess what's in it. Throw mango in your salsa, peanut butter in your stew, and attitude into every stir.
According to food psychologist Paul Rozin, experimentation with chilli actually builds resilience, not just physically, but emotionally (Rozin et al., 2013). That means your chilli game is literally making you stronger.

Who knew your Saturday night samosa test run was therapy?

3. May You Feed More Than Mouths

Food has always been the original love language. But spicy food? That's like the romantic poetry version—hot, messy, unforgettable.
So, whether you're feeding guests, family, or yourself after a long, soul-punching week, remember: what you're really offering is care. Fire is the seasoning. But connection? That's the main course.

A 2018 study from *Appetite* journal found that meals shared with emotional intention increase both mood and relational trust (Dunbar, 2018). Translation: when you cook with love (and heat), people taste both.

So, cook like someone's crying, healing, laughing, or falling in love at your table. Because someone probably is.

Final Words from the Sorceress

I won't end with "goodbye." I hate goodbyes. They're cold. And this book never once played it cold.

So instead, I say: keep the flame alive. Keep that bottle of sriracha close. Keep dancing in your kitchen with sambal on your shirt. Keep turning strangers into friends with nothing more than tacos and boldness.

You, my flame-hearted reader, are now officially anointed in the Order of the Pepper. Wear your crown of capsaicin with pride. And if someone ever asks you what this whole "chilli cookbook" thing was all about?
Smile, wink, and say, "It was hot. It was hilarious. And it changed how I cook forever."

ABOUT THE AUTHOR

Nancy Hillary has spent over three decades immersed in the world of music, touring, and live entertainment, shaping the pulse of stages across continents. Raised between England and South Africa, her childhood was rooted in self-sufficient farm life, where creativity, cooking, and gardening were daily rituals led by her spirited mother. Now based in Sydney, Nancy turned lockdown into a launchpad—digging into the soil, the spice rack, and her own stories. Entertaining With Chillies is the fiery first release under her Chilli Sorceress label, born from passion, play, and more than a few chilli-induced kitchen mishaps.

BIBLIOGRAPHY

Almeida, R. (2020). *Malagueta madness: Heat in Brazilian kitchens. Global Pepper Journal, 5.*

Avery. (2023). *How to create waterproof labels at home.* https://www.avery.com

Bajaj, K. L., & Kaur, G. (1981). Capsaicin content and pungency of chillies as affected by different drying methods. *Plant Foods for Human Nutrition, 31*(3), 287–291.

Bajwa, U., et al. (2021). Alternative cooling agents for capsaicin sensitivity in non-dairy consumers. *International Journal of Culinary Therapy, 7*(4), 88–94.

Barham, P. (2001). *The science of cooking.* Springer.

BBC News. (2022). *Man eats 17 ghost peppers in 60 seconds.* https://www.bbc.com/news

BBC Travel. (2023). *How Brazil eats feijoada.* https://www.bbc.com/travel

Bennett, R., & Stokes, L. (2020). Soothing the Scoville: The role of casein in capsaicin relief. *Food Chemistry Today, 11*(1), 44–50.

Bittencourt, J. (2019). *Feijoada & folklore: The food of the Brazilian soul.* São Paulo Culinary House.

Bley, K., Boorman, G., Mohammad, B., McKenzie, D., & Babbar, S. (2012). Safety and efficacy of capsaicin and capsaicin creams: A review of the literature. *Food and Chemical Toxicology, 50*(9), 3105–3114.

Bon Appétit Magazine. (2021). *What the heck is chimichurri, and why you should be making it?*

Bosland, P. W. (1996). Capsicums: Innovative uses of an ancient crop. *Progress in New Crops,* 479–487.

Bosland, P. W., & Baral, J. B. (2007). Biological properties of capsaicin and its analogs. *Journal of Ethnopharmacology, 108*(3), 421–432.

Bosland, P. W., & Votava, E. J. (2012). *Peppers: Vegetable and spice capsicums* (2nd ed.). CABI.

British Nutrition Foundation. (2021). *Enjoying spicy foods safely.*

Bryant, A., & Mezine, L. (2021). The neurogastronomy of Sichuan cuisine. *Journal of Culinary Science.*

Bryant, J., Moreno, K., & Taylor, S. (2021). Pain, pleasure, and peppers: A study of extreme spice endurance. *Journal of Culinary Science & Technology, 19*(2), 113–127.

Byrnes, N. K., & Hayes, J. E. (2013). Personality factors predict spicy food liking and intake. *Food Quality and Preference, 28*(1), 213–221.

Canva. (2024). *Label design templates.* https://www.canva.com

Caterina, M. J., Schumacher, M. A., Tominaga, M., Rosen, T. A., Levine, J. D., & Julius, D. (1997). The capsaicin receptor: A heat-activated ion channel in the pain pathway. *Nature, 389*(6653), 816–824.

Chang, D., & Meehan, P. (2018). *Eat a peach.* Clarkson Potter.

Chakraborty, M. (2021). *The magical beliefs behind Nimbu-Mirchi charms.* Cultural India Press.

CNN. (2010). *India to use world's hottest chili in weapons.*

Drewnowski, A., & Gomez-Carneros, C. (2000). Bitter taste, phytonutrients, and the consumer: A review. *The American Journal of Clinical Nutrition, 72*(6), 1424–1435.

Dunlop, F. (2006). *Revolutionary Chinese cookbook: Recipes from Hunan Province.* W. W. Norton & Company.

Dunlop, F. (2019). *The food of Sichuan.* W. W. Norton & Company.

El-Wakil, Y. (2021). *Middle Eastern heat: A culinary journey through spice and soul.* Sand & Spice Books.

Ford, L., Smith, A., & Chong, R. (2022). Spice sensitivity and party dynamics: What hosts should know. *Journal of Food and Social Studies.*

Garcia, M. (2022). What to do when spicy food strikes back. *Gastro Central Journal.*

Govindarajan, V. S. (1985). Capsicum, production, technology, chemistry, and quality. *Critical Reviews in Food Science & Nutrition, 22*(2), 109–176.

Gupta, M. (2019). *The science of spirits and spices.* Bartender's Manual Press.

Hoffman, R. J., Biederman, R. D., & Vlahov, D. (2016). Capsaicin toxicity: Hot peppers and a burning mouth. *Journal of Emergency Medicine,*

51(1), 104–106.

Hot Sauce Magazine. (2020). *Why we like the burn: A study on spice and satisfaction.*

Kim, H., & Lee, Y. (2020). *Fermented flavour: The Korean guide to spicy cuisine.* Seoul Food Press.

Kinnamon, S. C. (2012). Taste receptor signaling: Calcium, cAMP, and phosphatidylinositol pathways. *Current Opinion in Neurobiology, 22*(3), 401–407.

Kobata, K. (2014). Capsaicin and the human pain response. *Neuroscience Letters, 561,* 72–76.

Korea Food Promotion Institute. (2020). *Cultural heritage foods of Korea.*

Krishna, A. (2012). *Customer sense: How the 5 senses influence buying behavior.* Palgrave Macmillan.

Kurlansky, M. (2002). *Salt: A world history.* Vintage.

League of Fire. (2022). *Chilli-eating competitions and rankings.* https://leagueoffire.com

Lemoine, M. (2018). *The soul of chimichurri: Argentina's national treasure.* Mendoza Culinary Press.

Ludy, M. J., & Mattes, R. D. (2011). The effects of hedonically acceptable red pepper doses on thermogenesis and appetite. *Physiology & Behavior, 102*(3), 251–258.

Lv, J., et al. (2015). Consumption of spicy foods and total and cause specific mortality: Population-based cohort study. *The BMJ.* https://www.bmj.com/content/351/bmj.h3942

Mann, D., Rao, N., & Patel, R. (2020). *Flavours of India: Modern spice pairings.* Masala House Press.

Mashhadi, N. S., Ghiasvand, R., Askari, G., Hariri, M., Darvishi, L., & Mofid, M. R. (2013). Anti-oxidative and anti-inflammatory effects of ginger in health and physical activity: Review of current evidence. *International Journal of Preventive Medicine, 4*(Suppl 1), S36.

McGee, H. (2004). *On food and cooking: The science and lore of the kitchen.* Scribner.

Mendoza, L. (2022). *Tropic heat: Fruits that love spice.* Latin Flavour Publishing.

Muñoz, J. (2020). Chancho en piedra and the magic of cacho de cabra. *Revista del Sabor.*

NASA. (2021). *NASA astronaut harvests first ever chile peppers grown in space.* https://www.nasa.gov/feature/nasa-astronaut-harvests-first-ever-chile-peppers-grown-in-space

Oseland, J. (2010). *Cradle of flavor: Home cooking from the Spice Islands of Indonesia.* W. W. Norton.

Peterson, J. (2022). Layering heat: The rise of chilli in mixology. *Global Bartending Trends, 14*(1), 33–41.

Pickersgill, B. (2007). Domestication of plants in the Americas: The origin of chilli peppers. *Economic Botany, 61*(1), 68–78.

Pilcher, J. (2012). *Planet taco: A global history of Mexican food.* Oxford University Press.

Prescott, J. (2015). Multidimensional analysis of spicy food liking: Taste, heat, and personality. *Food Quality and Preference, 39*, 8–15.

Prescott, J., & Stevenson, R. J. (1996). Psychophysics of taste and smell in food acceptance. *Food Quality and Preference, 7*(4), 217–224.

Ravikumar, S., & Kathirvel, B. (2020). Traditional uses of capsicum and its pharmacological properties. *Journal of Ethnopharmacology, 251.*

Rozin, P., & Schiller, D. (1980). The nature and acquisition of a preference for chili pepper by humans. *Motivation and Emotion, 4*(1), 77–101.

Rozin, P., Guillot, L., Fincher, K., Rozin, A., & Tsukayama, E. (2013). Cultural and individual differences in the elicitation of disgust. *Emotion Review, 5*(3), 230–234.

Scoville, W. L. (1912). Note on capsicums. *Journal of the American Pharmacists Association, 1*(5), 453.

Shepherd, G. M. (2006). Smell images and the flavour system in the human brain. *Nature, 444*(7117), 316–321.

Shurtleff, W., & Aoyagi, A. (2012). *The book of miso.* Ten Speed Press.

Smith, A. (2014). *American food: A not-so-serious history.* University of Chicago Press.

Spence, C. (2015). *Gastrophysics: The new science of eating.* Viking.

Spence, C. (2015). Multisensory flavor perception. *Cell, 161*(1), 24–35.

Stevenson, R. J. (2009). *The psychology of flavour.* Oxford University Press.

Szabo, L. (2015). Global chili pastes: Flavour, fire and fermentation. *Culinary Science Quarterly, 3*(1), 38–45.

Tan, V. M. H., & Lee, J. (2017). Gochujang and fermented chilli pastes: Hot stuff in nutrition. *Journal of Ethnic Foods, 4*(4), 204–209.

Tamang, J. P., et al. (2016). *Fermented foods and beverages of the world.* CRC Press.

Tapsell, L. C., Hemphill, I., Cobiac, L., Patch, C. S., Sullivan, D. R., Fenech, M., ... & Inge, K. E. (2006). Health benefits of herbs and spices: The past, the present, the future. *Medical Journal of Australia, 185*(4), S4–S24.

Tolbert, F. X. (1966). *A bowl of red.* Doubleday.

Valdés, A., & Riquelme, M. (2019). *Chilean hot: The spice cultures of the Andes.* Ediciones Sur.

Willet, B. (2015). *Hot sauce nation: America's burning obsession.* Overlook Press.

Yanti, L. (2021). Sambal: More than just heat. *Indonesia Culinary Review.*

Yoshioka, M., Doucet, E., & Tremblay, A. (2004). Spicy food and satiety: A potential metabolic advantage. *Appetite, 42*(2), 149–154.

Zandstra, E. H., de Graaf, C., & Van Trijp, H. C. M. (2016). Eating at the table: The influence of atmospherics on the social and emotional responses to food. *Appetite, 103,* 116–123.

Zhang, H., Liu, J., & Chen, Q. (2019). Speedy meals and culinary hacks. *Modern Eats Review, 7*(2), 102–109.